The Roots of a Dream

A spiritual journey in the steps of Don Bosco

I am happy to introduce this original work to you.

The Roots of a Dream will allow you to rediscover a scent and an atmosphere that are charged with memories and emotions. But it will do more than this; it will invite you to adjust your pace to that of Don Bosco. His simple steps were measured against the yardstick of charity and guided by a single ambition: holiness, wherever it could be achieved.

This book is not a biography; nor is it a guide. It is rather a meditation on a child who became a man and who, with his joys and sorrows, his doubts and his deep convictions, would become a saint in the service of a mission. This mission was to witness to the love of God for young people.

In this book you will see a different Don Bosco, one who is close to you because he is deeply human. We can discuss whether or not he thought or experienced this or that, but we can be in no doubt about his deep humanity that makes him so close to us. It is this closeness that the book tries to reproduce in an attempt to invite us to move forward into a fruitful future. And to convince us of this, it confronts us too with present-day situations, showing us that we can take our inspiration from his way of doing things. For to set our feet in the footsteps of Don Bosco means first and foremost trying to share in what made his life tick. He spent his time pulling children and young people out of the shadows and into the light of the Risen Christ. And this is the path that Don Bosco wants to lead us along. I wish to say a big thank-you to the authors. May the following pages go some way to inciting the reader to follow such a path.

Pascual Chávez V.

Fr Pascual Chávez Villanueva
Ninth Successor to Don Bosco

Saint John Bosco 1815–1888

John Bosco was born on 16 August 1815 in a hamlet known as The Becchi not far from Turin.
The Napoleonic wars were finally over. He lived with his parents Francis and Margaret, his two older
brothers and his paternal grandmother also named Margaret. John was less than two years old when his father,
a farm worker, died of pneumonia. Margaret Bosco had three youngsters and a sick mother-in-law to care for,
five mouths to feed and little money coming in – these were hard times for the Bosco family.
John was about nine years old when he had a dream that he would talk about for the rest of his life.
It seemed to be telling him that he was called by God to be a priest. When John was fourteen he started to learn
Latin from his parish priest, who also helped him to develop a life of faith. At twenty he finally went
to the seminary in Chieri, and six years later, on the 5 June 1841, he was ordained a priest.

As a priest, his work was vast and varied: visiting prisoners, providing lodgings for street children,
building churches, writing and publishing books both for young people and for adults.
Some were history books; others taught the Catholic faith.
In 1859 he already had a group of young men around him, and with them he founded a new religious congregation
which they called The Salesians, after St Francis de Sales. In 1872, together with Mary Domenica Mazzarello, he founded
a similar congregation for young women, who became known as The Salesian Sisters.
In 1876 he also set up an association for lay people; these he called The Salesian Cooperators.
A year earlier, he had already sent some of his Salesians from Italy to work for young people in France and South America.

By the time he died, on 31 January 1888, his Salesian family was flourishing and growing rapidly.
He was canonised by Pius XI in 1934.
In January 1988 – one hundred years after his death – Pope John Paul II called him Father and Teacher of Youth.

A spiritual journey begins

It is said that our native place makes us what we are. This was true of Don Bosco, born into a poor peasant family on the Piedmont slopes. He spent his youth on a farm, where he worked and lived on the fruits of the earth.

Later, as a priest working for young people in the heart of the city of Turin, he lived out a life far beyond anything that his rural origins could have predicted. Imagine the life of a tree, with its roots plunged deep into the earth and its branches reaching up to the sky. Don Bosco, who had suffered in Turin under the dark, leaden clouds of the painful beginnings of the industrial revolution, was determined to open up brighter horizons for its young people and give them genuine reason for hope in a better future.

In this book we follow in the footsteps of Don Bosco, discover the places and experiences that shaped his life, not just to understand his story, but rather to discover the human and spiritual dynamism that shapes anyone who is passionate about life. In trying to understand his life, we may be helped to understand our own lives.

The reader is invited to retrace the life of Don Bosco, to journey, with him, through the pleasant hills of Piedmont and the bustling city of Turin. In understanding what happened to Don Bosco, it is to be hoped that readers will begin to understand the influences and experiences which shape their own lives. In appreciating all that Don Bosco did for young people in need, the reader may be inspired to follow in his footsteps.

The Becchi

The Becchi is made up of eight to ten little homes scattered along the ridge of one of those slight waves of ground that rib the plain beyond Chieri. A few farm-labourers' cottages, the villa of a well-heeled country landowner, a few fields running down the slopes, a communal kiln in front of the group of houses, and as far as the eye can see, wooded hills which provide a safe shelter for deserters from Napoleon's armies.– Such was the appearance of the village. – Opposite, on a tongue of land which cuts off the horizon to the east, the belfry of Buttigliera dominates the landscape like a finger pointing heavenwards.

This landscape, so well described by biographers of Don Bosco in the last century, is much the same today. There is, of course, the sanctuary dedicated to Don Bosco, known as The Temple, which towers over the humble scene below. It may seem a little out of place, but we must not forget that that this is the place where John Bosco experienced the hard life of the rural peasants, poor but supportive of each other. Among the families, from one house to another, so many acts of kindness were done. The generosity of Don Bosco's own mother often went far beyond good neighbourliness. She would discreetly take a bowl of soup to someone ostracised by the rest. Often she gave hospitality to beggars, and even provided food and a heap of straw for army deserters hiding in the neighbouring woods. None of that would have gone unnoticed by the young John Bosco. This was his apprenticeship in loving-kindness and an added feature of beauty in this rural scene.

This was my home

- *Come on, Don Bosco, where is your house?*
- *Not far to go now. It's just after the next bend. You'll see the roof.*

The young priest's teasing did not satisfy the youngsters, who could not wait to get there.

What a treat it was for them each autumn to leave the outskirts of Turin and set out for Don Bosco's Home! There was always a hard struggle with their employers to negotiate these few days off, but for these young apprentice masons, stone-cutters, wood-workers, and labourers, nothing in the world would have tempted them to miss this outing. For Don Bosco, too, this was a treasured event. The great outdoors, the hills of the Becchi, dinner with chestnuts, the barn loaned by his brother Joseph – all this was just what they needed.

- *Tell us about your brother Joseph. Does he look like you?*
- *Just wait and see. And, by the way, he's stronger than I am!*
- *And what about the other – the awkward one?*

- *What do you mean – awkward? It wasn't easy for him, you know. Like you, he lost his mother when he was young. And when our father married again, Anthony had very little more time with him. I was less than two years old when father died, so Tony had to do most of the work. Naturally he wanted to be the boss, but I didn't let it bother me.*

Don Bosco never tired of telling those young orphans about his early life – tidbits of family history to compensate for what life had denied them.

- *Don Bosco, I can see it! There it is!* And like a flock of sparrows, they were off! Don Bosco, not to be outdone, hitched up his cassock and joined the chase. His honour was at stake – he would beat them over the distance. He knew the slope – and its pitfalls – all too well. The dogs came out to meet them.
- *Three cheers for Don Bosco,* they shouted.

A breathless Don Bosco had led the pack
-*This is my home!* said Don Bosco to his wide-eyed audience, revealing not an

enchanted castle, but a poor wooden structure – a barn! The boys who had been there before exchanged knowing looks – it really would be home for them for a few days. By nightfall, amid the smell of hay and the warmth of the earth, each youngster began to appreciate the home where Don Bosco had been a child.

house where Don Bosco spent his childhood

A home for each one

You loved to say, *Questa è la mia casa,*
This is my home,
pointing to your house.
A tumbledown cottage, a shed, a shack.
A kitchen and two bedrooms. A barn and a stable.
But for you, it was a palace in the Becchi kingdom.
How many *Don Bosco Homes* you've built!
But this one is forever your home,
an image of all that children need:
family and food on the table.
A home where each one counted,
where the homeless poor were always welcome.
The home you had to leave behind,
driven out by an older brother's jealous anger.
The home where, at the end of the day,
there was always enough to eat,
the daily bead, earned by the sweat of each one.
Don Bosco, you never forgot your roots.
You came here on pilgrimage to tread the family turf.
Your humble spirit seasons your sanctity.
You were the first to gaze in wonder
at what God brought about through you.
Don Bosco, your great heart is large enough
to be a home for all children in need.
The youngsters of the Pinardi shed could say,
like Mary's Child,
This is our manger, our Bethlehem.
Thousands of young people can now say of Valdocco:
Questa è la mia casa.
And throughout the world today,
millions of children,
from the shacks of Brazil to the schools of Japan,
can say: *This is my home.*

Thank you for all those who have found a new life
in your home.

The Land and its people

What is this land where the Bosco family has its roots – the scenery that surrounded John as he grew up; the air he breathed; the people he mingled with; his birthplace and its surroundings; the scene of his growing years, with all the painful struggles, the comings and goings – the place where he gave so much of himself?

This land is Piedmont, a fertile plain of cereal crops and grazing cattle, and all around the vine-covered hills. In the far distance, to the north, are the snowy peaks of the Alps. Cascading down the slopes is a series of lakes, then a torrent which becomes the river Po, whose waters irrigate the whole of northern Italy.

Its people, shaped and moulded by migrations of people from North and South, are hard-working and talented in a variety of trades: masons, glass-makers, artistic designers, but often compelled to pull up their roots and use their skills elsewhere in the world in order to make a living.

As a people, tested and toughened by their turbulent history, the Piedmontese are level-headed, practical and down-to-earth. Though they can be calm, unruffled and tenacious, at the same time they know how to enjoy life and have their own brand of humour.

The Piedmontese family is strongly united, deeply religious, not without a touch of superstition, committed to daily prayer, and able to confront death with serenity. Their piety is natural and quite unselfconscious, built on an unshakeable trust in Divine Providence. The father is the master of the household and uses his authority to hold his family together. To live and to work together could well be the Piedmontese motto.

This was the land, these were its people at the time when John Bosco was born, grew up and lived out his life.

The good smell of the earth!

What a great paradox: John Bosco, the boy with deep peasant roots, destined to spend his life for young people in one of the largest cities in the north of Italy! Doesn't it make you wonder when you go through the Becchi museum of peasant life?

But it's only an apparent paradox.

From his closeness to the soil John Bosco inherited rock-solid common sense, a pragmatic approach to problems and a toughness of character that would serve him well all through his life.

Just as he had to cope with the rugged earth, so he would have to deal with the harshness of industrialised, 19th-century city life. This would be a preparation for, rather than a threat to his vocation. Think of the patience of the peasant farmer who waits for the seed to germinate. Perseverance, too: there are no short cuts in farming. If plants and animals are to grow, despite the hazards of weather, strength of purpose is required. All these qualities would be needed in his life and work with the young. They are basic to education. To educate is to promote growth.

In any case, the youngsters he would have to deal with in Turin came from that same peasant world as he did. They were children from families who had hoped to find an alternative to the poor, sparse living they had in the country. Most of the time all they found was the wretched, grinding work of the factories. The workshops, the mills needed child labour and paid pitiful wages which left families with little choice.

Soon the long weary hours broke them and these unfortunate children ended up on the streets.

Beyond the picture of country life seen in the many museum artifacts and photos, sense the smell of the earth that would never leave the nostrils of young John Bosco, like something clinging to the soles of his feet. His native soil. A modest identity he would never disown.

My Land

The land of our childhood calls us,
Grounds us in time and place,
Clings to our feet, fills our senses,
Stays with us, all our days.

Smell of cooking, songs on the radio,
Our streets, our parks, our playing fields
Echoing with a powerful call,
Still shape us, all our days.

Buried in those early years
Treasures of challenges and talents
Mapped from the past to our present lives
To be discovered, every day.

In Don Bosco beat a country heart
For the poor outcasts of Turin.
From his own land he drew the lessons
Enriching children, all their days.

Our land, with childhood roots,
Good and bad,
Calls each of us to unearth the riches
Buried in our gifts and our experiences,
Treasures to be, all our days.

The Becchi

Turin

Congress of Vienna

Cavour

16

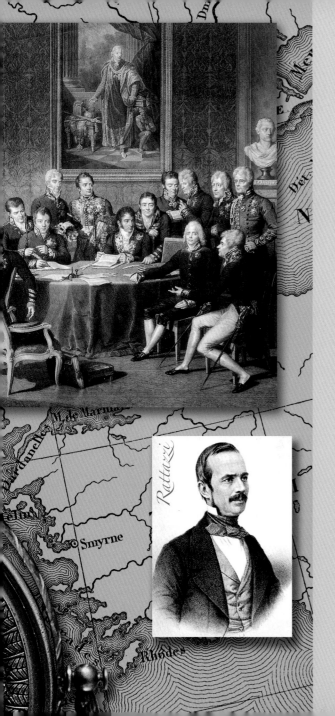

Turbulent time

The historical and political environment in which John Bosco lived and worked was more of a raging torrent than a tranquil river. A few important dates stand out in this rather troubled period.

1815. The year of John Bosco's birth sees the Congress of Vienna. Napoleon abdicates, but attempts to regain power only to see his empire collapse with his defeat at the Battle of Waterloo. The big powers divide Europe among themselves. Italy becomes a great jigsaw puzzle of states, kingdoms and principalities. Refugees hounded by the police find hospitality in the Bosco home. John will always remember that.

1848. The French Revolution has become contagious. Countries are aspiring to draft their own laws. The major cities of Europe ignite, only to provoke reprisals. Some want to set up a parliamentary system. Others fight for a real independence from the Austrian Empire, which includes Northern Italy. Piedmont is at war.

1861. The Kingdom of Italy is created. Cavour, a member of the Turin parliament, will be the linchpin of Italian unity. He stands for liberal policies. Once he becomes President of the Council of Piedmont, he negotiates with Napoleon III, offering military support to drive the Austrians from the peninsula. After a few political somersaults, and following Napoleon's signing of an armistice, he resigns – but before long he will return to power.

Though not directly involved in political affairs, Don Bosco was able to make and sustain contacts with people in high government office, all to the advantage of his various establishments. His work was much appreciated by the government minister Rattazzi, especially when he saw how Don Bosco's older pupils tended the sick during the cholera epidemic, and also when Don Bosco organised an outing for young prisoners. It was also Rattazzi who would urge Don Bosco to found a society that would continue his work after him. He would even show Don Bosco how to get around the law that was already suppressing many religious orders.

17

A child's dream

The three children had been asleep for a while in the bedroom they shared above the stable at the Becchi farm. Before long their mother Margaret came up to the bedroom opposite, which she shared with her mother-in-law, [also] Margaret [Zucca], but not before having a last look around downstairs and outside to check that there were no prowlers.

- *Everything quiet down there?* whispered the grandmother.
- *Not asleep yet, mum?*
- *No. I've been thinking about the dream John told us about this morning.*
- *Strange tale!*
- *But you told him not to pay any heed to dreams.*
- *Yes … for a bit of peace in the house. You saw for yourself how Anthony reacted: You'll be leader of a gang of robbers. It doesn't take much to annoy him.*

Mamma Margaret often had to intervene between her youngest and the oldest boy. That morning, in fact, John had come down all dishevelled, complaining that he was sore all over, as if he'd been fighting all night. His brothers were annoyed with him for being restless and keeping them awake. Then John began to tell them about this dream. A strange dream, about a group of young people, fighting and swearing, and John weighing in with his fists to stop them.

He was losing from the start; but before it became a complete disaster the group suddenly changed into wild, wolf-like animals. At the same time a man appeared, bathed in light, who began to talk to John. He took him aside and led him towards a woman of great beauty and radiance, saying that she was his mother. She asked John to change these wolves into peaceful lambs, saying that he must do it using gentle, not violent ways. Overcome by the mystery of it all, John burst into tears, and at that point he woke up. Hearing this story, his brother Joseph was quite excited, but his half-brother Anthony was just irritated by it all.

- *Maybe he'll become a priest,* whispered his mother.
- *Margaret, a Bosco becoming a priest, never!* said the mother–in-law. *Nobody in your family or mine could ever afford his studies. Teach them all the fear of God, and they'll make good husbands and fathers. Good night.*

Both women offered up a quiet prayer before lapsing into sleep at the end of another tiring day.

From dream to reality

Wouldn't any one of us like to have such a strong vision of our vocation to point the way ahead?

Unfortunately, discernment is rarely so simple and clear, and so we often stagger this way and that in our efforts to be sure of our call. With no clear indication of our future to guide us, we can still have our dreams. Dreams with our eyes open, which allow us to move around, test the waters, take initiatives, project ourselves into the future. We could lose ourselves in that and simply enjoy the adventure, or we can actually see our future taking shape. Every dream, of course, needs a reality check: dream and realism wisely balanced. It's a journey from earth to heaven, from our roots to our loftiest achievements, from the here and now to the better future we want for ourselves and for others. If we retrace the journey Don Bosco made, it can inspire our own dreams and anchor us firmly in a genuine love of God and of others.

A catechist in the making

It's just amazing! Everybody's here! How many can I count today? About forty. I can see my big brother Joseph there, his eyes sparkling with pride, sitting with the others on the grass. All the young people I know in the village are here – their parents too. I can feel the excitement rising in me. Today I've promised them that I'll do a tight-rope walk. I've spent hours practising to be an acrobat after I've finished my day's work. All in secret, of course, so as to make it a surprise, and especially to avoid Anthony's snide remarks – he's my eldest half-brother. He thinks it's a waste of time and will just make me big-headed. But you can be sure that if I pull it off, he'll go around boasting about it among his pals. I try to learn from watching the professionals when we go to the market as a family to sell some of our produce. I'm not as strong as they are, but working in the fields keeps me fit. Apart from that it's just a matter of practise, know-how and determination. The rope is strong and reliable, and my mother secretly encourages me. She's delighted with our Sunday afternoon gatherings. We always end with a prayer – she insists on it, because, as she says, *"We have to thank the good God that we have a life here on earth"*.

- Anything new for us today, John?

That's Gino, one of our neighbours – a good friend who is a kind of publicity agent for me around the area. He's my biggest fan, even if he does go a bit over the top. With his quick wit, he added a touch of novelty to my act. He's the one I put questions to when I come to the part where I talk about what we heard at Mass that morning. He calls me his 'Little parish priest!'

- Gino, you see the rope here? He scratches his head and looks amazed…

- John! Do want to kill yourself? If all you want is to give us a laugh, it isn't worth it.

- No, I'm not going to kill myself. But get them to say a prayer just to make sure! Gino promptly calms them all down. I can see my mother keeping a low profile among friends from her native village. Suppose the Little Priest of the Becchi could make Gino his first curate! That would be my greatest triumph!

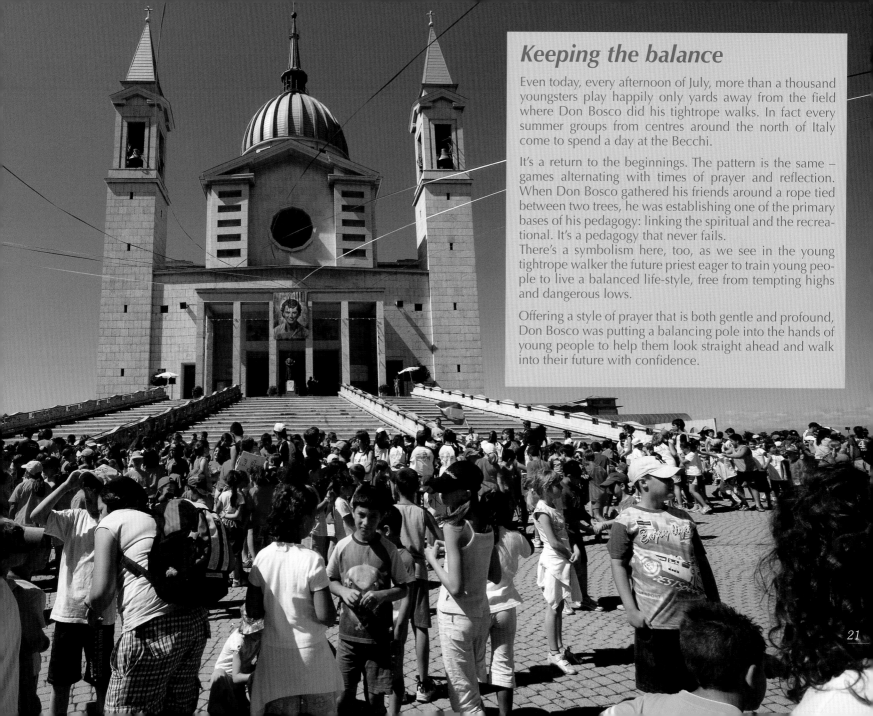

Keeping the balance

Even today, every afternoon of July, more than a thousand youngsters play happily only yards away from the field where Don Bosco did his tightrope walks. In fact every summer groups from centres around the north of Italy come to spend a day at the Becchi.

It's a return to the beginnings. The pattern is the same – games alternating with times of prayer and reflection. When Don Bosco gathered his friends around a rope tied between two trees, he was establishing one of the primary bases of his pedagogy: linking the spiritual and the recreational. It's a pedagogy that never fails.

There's a symbolism here, too, as we see in the young tightrope walker the future priest eager to train young people to live a balanced life-style, free from tempting highs and dangerous lows.

Offering a style of prayer that is both gentle and profound, Don Bosco was putting a balancing pole into the hands of young people to help them look straight ahead and walk into their future with confidence.

The Lord's acrobat

You were a labourer's son,
The Lord's acrobat;
Child of the earth and of the seasons,
Son of the sowing and the reaping.

For someone who has never suffered
Poverty is a closed book.
To gather in, you must sow.
John Bosco, you gave all.

Brothers and sisters, of one mind and heart.
God will be there on the road beside you
Till the end of time.

In the sun, in the dust,
Trusting in the goodness of God,
Pillar amongst the little ones,
The orphans, the penniless,
When the wheat was dry and dead
You prayed to the Immaculate.
With two grains to make four ears of corn
God gave meaning to your life.

Into the hands of the Madonna,
Loving Mother of the poor,
You entrusted your future:
You are the wood of her ship.
Hills of Asti,
Remember for years to come
The feet that walked in wooden clogs,
The heart full of joy.

This bronze piece near
Don Bosco's home is the work
of the Roman sculptor
Ennio Tessei.

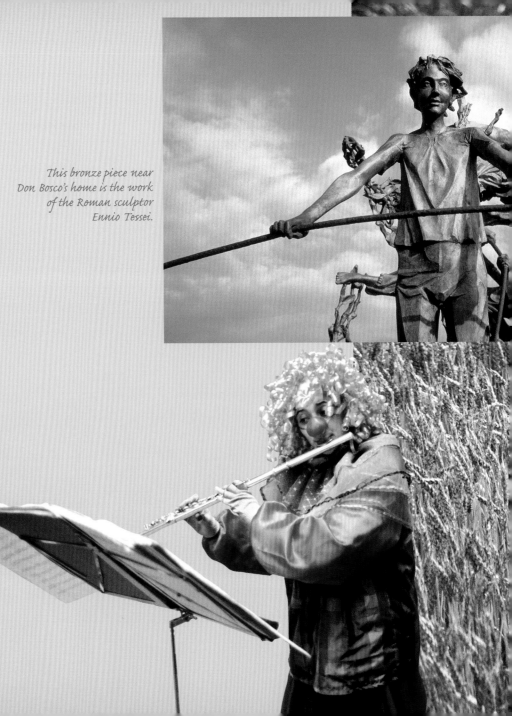

22

A sad separation

My mind feels all confused. I've been wandering around the countryside since this morning, going from farm to farm, hoping to be taken on as a cowherd. But nobody seems to want me. To begin with, I went to the neighbouring farms, but they all gave the same answer: *Sorry, John. If you came in the spring, I wouldn't refuse. But now, in the middle of February, there's no work. I've even sent my own workers away. What's been happening at your house?*

I grabbed my meagre bundle of clothes and left without a word. When I reached the bend in the road my eyes were sore: was it from tears from a heavy heart, or from the icy wind that whipped my face? I don't remember my father, who died when I was less than two years old, and here I am now forced to leave my mother and my two brothers. Tough when you're only twelve. *For the sake of peace in the home, I'm asking you to leave. Here, take your pack of clothes – two shirts and two hankies – and go to the Bausone farm. They'll have some work for you there.* I embraced my

mother and set out. I was free, but full of bitterness. It's true that this move could open up a chance to carry out what I'd planned: find work and go ahead with studies for the priesthood, without the endless insults from Anthony. He really does act like the boss. But nobody seems to want to know me! It's an unfair world. How many times I've helped these people – at the markets, in the fields, and never begrudging the time it took. *You have to give, John, give with a good heart.* That's what I learned from my mother…. I can't stand this freezing cold.

Dogs bark when I get near houses. Even the sky seems to weep as I cry out to God. This one is the Moglia farm. It's already dark, but again it's the same answer: *There's no work here!* John Bosco, the acrobat from the Becchi, collapses in the snow.

Good people, take pity on him! If he becomes a man, thanks to you, he will lift thousands from the gutter. Lend him a hand, give him food and lodging. Believe in him. Let today's misery become tomorrow's memory.

The Moglia farm today

Knowing you are loved

When he was only twelve, John Bosco had to leave his mother and live away from home for two years because the atmosphere there made life impossible for him. For his mother it was a regrettable choice made in the hope of something better: she needed time for it to blow over and settle down. John would, in fact, be able to go back and follow his dream of studying for the priesthood, but it was a difficult time for him; a real suffering that he had to overcome.

There are many children and teenagers today who have to grow up away from home because, for some reason or other, their parents can't cope. As one expert in education says: It isn't that children are difficult; it's more a question of the hard road they've been forced to travel. Suffering knows no age limits. Even very young children are not spared. Their hurts can have many sources, but when grown-ups cause them, it's a real scandal.

It's clear that children and teenagers are vulnerable people. They can put up with a great deal, but sometimes they are inclined just to give up, even to the point of attempting suicide.

How important it is to ensure that they don't see their life as meaningless, with no future, that they are alone in the world, and that life will either pass them by or even pull them down.

John Bosco was one such wounded child, but he became a priest and devoted his whole life to numberless children at risk. Our own experience in education also shows us that no one's life is a dead-end; that even the youngest children, in spite of their hurts, can find ways to move on, regain their self-confidence and follow a good career.

There is one thing above all else that can make this possible: knowing that they are loved.

25

The presence of a father figure

It was early evening in November 1829, and we were hurrying to get home before dark. The chilly breeze caught us as we rounded the bend in the road. My brothers Joseph and Anthony were with their friends, and further ahead my mother was with a group of women, praying the rosary. The men were joining in, a bit distracted as their eyes roamed over the countryside. For three days we'd been going back and forth between the Becchi and the next village to listen to the sermons at the parish mission*. There was a good turnout. It was an important event, and we wanted to give it our best. I was walking on my own, away from the rest. I felt quite excited. Everything I'd been hearing made me want to know more about God. I was hearing new things that touched me deeply, yet I seemed to grasp them easily. If only I could put across the same teaching to my friends! But there was one big problem: that mule-head of a brother, Anthony. Whenever he saw me with books, he just went crazy. I was fourteen, with a head full of wild dreams! But if I was ever to be able to speak like a priest, I had to study, and there seemed little chance of that as

I went around looking for someone to teach me in the winter months. I was getting desperate, and there seemed to be no way out. I walked on in silence, mulling over my frustration.

Just then, Don Calosso, the new chaplain from nearby Morialdo, came up to me. He was a stooped seventy-year-old and looked a little weary, but I sensed right away that he was a wise and holy man. He questioned me briefly about what I'd understood at the mission, and I was able to repeat for him the two sermons I'd heard. I also told him that I was eager to get some schooling. He showed me great kindness, and that gave me hope. He actually spoke to my mother, and the following Sunday I was having my first lessons with him. From then on, he was my guide and mentor, and I began to learn about living a spiritual life. His first name was Melchior – my name, too! We were just made to get on well with each other. He became a real father to me – the father I'd been cruelly deprived of for so long … All praise to the God of the humble and the lowly!

*mission: a parish retreat with various priests coming from elsewhere

26

The A

...nlet of Buttigliera, seen from the Becchi. Below : the church of Morialdo where Don Calosso ministered.

Someone you can count on

When we were young there were people we could count on – parents, a teacher, a relative, an older brother or sister. They may not have been perfect models for us; they were just there when we needed them for a little support or a word of encouragement. With them around, we didn't avoid problems, but they did help us to work through them and put them behind us. They also helped us to have sound views of life and the real world.

Thanks to all these people we learned to face challenges. Through them we discovered our own self-worth at a time when we could easily have lost it. We also learned that you just can't 'go it alone', and that we are blessed in knowing we can count on others.

On our journey into manhood or womanhood, when we were discouraged or losing our way, they were there, and with their helping hands we were able to grow up and get our lives together. It was their human kindness above all that enriched us. When, thanks to them, we got over the tricky stages of growing up and gained confidence, we began to see all the blind alleys that they helped us to avoid. What better way to show our gratitude than by becoming ourselves the kind of person that others can count on when the need arises?

Under the spotlight

It's Sunday 25 October 1835, and they're running out of places in the little church of Castelnuovo. People are coming in big numbers from neighbouring villages – the Becchi, Morialdo …. Young John Bosco is going to receive the cassock from Don Cinzano, the parish priest. Everybody wants to be there for the 'local boy'. A few years earlier the tailor, Master Giovanni Roberto, exclaimed: *Who put that idea into his head? He'll need to find ten thousand lire to become priest, but if he stays with me, he can earn a living and make a fresh start!* The young sixteen-year-old had come to him looking for lodgings for the winter, so as to avoid having to walk twenty kilometres a day, covering the distance between the Becchi and Castelnuovo four times over. Giovanni Roberto is also the parish organist. He's watching the crowds of people. He's not the only one to be showing his emotion.

The ceremony goes on, and as John takes off his layman's clothes, the parish priest says: *May the Lord strip you of the old man, with his former habits and ways.*
In the front row, his maternal grandfather Melchior Occhiena is very moved by all this. He remembers how, twenty years earlier, his daughter Margaret had come to ask him to be godfather to her second son. He himself had carried the tiny baby to the baptismal font. Many of the people in the congregation gave money to fit John Bosco out with cassock, hat, shoes, biretta and even his black socks. He will always be one of the poor to the end of his days. *May the Lord re-clothe you with the new man, created according to the heart of God, in justice, truth and holiness.* Near John's mother, Margaret, is Mrs Cafasso, whose son Joseph is a twenty-three-year-old priest already highly regarded as a spiritual director.

He's the one who encouraged John to enter the seminary, in spite of his agonising doubts. He even persuaded the rector of the seminary to waive John's fees for the first year.
Sixteen years later, 1 November 1851, Don Bosco comes back to this same church to preach the sermon for All Souls Day. Among the choirboys is a youngster watching Don Bosco closely.
- *Is there something you'd like to tell me?* asks Don Bosco.
- *Yes, Father. I would like to go with you to Turin to study and become a priest.*
Don Bosco takes the young orphan boy back with him. He knows all too well what life is like with no father and no money to spare. This young boy from Castelnuovo is John Cagliero, who will become the first Salesian Cardinal and founder of the Salesian Mission in South America.

The town of Castelnuovo and the parish church where Don Bosco was baptised.

Through the eyes of a child

Is there anything more fragile than a little child? He comes into the world naked, weak, defence-less, knowing nothing. He survives only through the love he is shown, the time spent to teach him to speak, to walk, to make his way a little in this world that meets his startled gaze.

Instinctively he's already equipped with essential know-how: how to feed, fight for himself. Just watch a young chicken, newly born and already trying to stand up on its two legs!

But how precious is his apprenticeship for life, as much for what he learns as for the affective environment in which he is taught. The first essential for this frail infant is his safety. That's why the parents need such foresight so that they can do their very best for him.

Besides, a good part of children's learning consists in imitating their parents or the adults around them. Logically, they want to be like those they admire. We can see, then, that in education it's more than just passing on knowledge and skills: children have to learn how to live. A child learns to see the world in the way he is taught to understand it and to live in it. This is what shapes his person. And if the adults among whom he grows up are people of living faith, he will want to know about faith, explore it, try it out, in order to be sure that he too can make it a valid support for his life. For us adults then, to live under the gaze of a child who is growing up is never meaningless, because through his questioning eyes he's trying to find out what life means for us.

29

A light from on high

The hill that the young John Bosco knew when he kept an eye on the family's cows is a far cry from the hill we see today. The gentle line of its slopes has been broken by the buildings that were erected there to honour him. As a modest peasant, he must be astounded at the idea, or maybe it just makes him smile. Today, as you make your way towards them, you can feel shocked by the severe shape of this 'Temple', as it's known. With its stark lines it seems to be an intrusive presence. It has to be said, all the same, that great numbers of pilgrims, including many youth groups, flock there every year from spring to autumn. Its grand, spacious facilities lend themselves well to joyful celebrations in memory of the shepherd boy of the Becchi, now glorious in God's presence.

When it was first built, the *Temple*, both inside and out, was a cold, oppressive mass of concrete. Renovation work has changed all that. Walk through one of its big, heavy doors, and you are in for a great surprise. Its lines are more gentle and rounded. Wood has covered the concrete, giving a warm feeling, and there is soft lighting.

The quiet atmosphere draws you into prayerful silence. The imposing figure of the risen Christ has been given a more fitting place: with his arms wide open he welcomes each one. The pilgrim is called to prayer; the curious visitor to a spiritual presence; the tourist to an uplifting place to rest a while. You could imagine yourself deep within a ship taking you on voyage of discovery. Christ is there, as he was in the dream at nine, when John Bosco saw a person of noble appearance showing him where his future mission would take him. Yes, it's the same Christ showing us, too, the way ahead. He invites us first of all to raise our eyes, because light comes from above.

He then moves us to look into ourselves, because this is a light that enlightens us with truth. Finally, he calls us to set out again from this hillside, strengthened and at peace, aware of all the good we still need to do. Don Bosco has had a share in this experience – there are frescoes that keep us mindful of him. He's counting on us to put our shoulders to the task: to make the whole world a Temple of the living God.

The Via Lucis

At the very heart of the Temple, the risen, glorious Christ holds out his arms as if to lead us to the Father. In line with this sculpture, along one side, where you might have expected to find a Way of the Cross, instead you find a Way of Light – the Via Lucis. Fourteen bas-reliefs, carved in luminous lime wood, tell of the amazing, extraordinary events that mark the fifty days between the Resurrection and the coming of the Holy Spirit at Pentecost. Though unusual, it's very fitting here. The Risen Christ reminds us of the power of God and what awaits us beyond death. In a world marked by sin and failure, Christ opens up a horizon of light and hope. Don Bosco, faced with young people crucified and without hope, was a witness of the love of God, the giver of hope. Education, for Don Bosco, is a work of redeeming love.

The fourteen stations of the Via Lucis

Jesus risen from the dead (Lk 24, 1-9); The empty tomb (Jn 20, 1-10); Jesus appears to Mary Magdalene (Mt 28, 1-9); Jesus with disciples on road to Emmaus (Lk 24, 13-27); Jesus recognised in the breaking of the bread (Lk 24, 28-32); Jesus appears to the disciples (Lk 24, 36-49); Jesus empowers his disciples to forgive sins (Jn 20, 19-23); Jesus confirms the faith of Thomas (Jn 20, 24-29); Jesus appears on the shore of Lake Tiberias (Jn 21, 1-14); Jesus confers the primacy on St Peter (Jn 21, 12-23); Jesus entrusts his disciples with his mission to the world (Mk 16, 14-20); Jesus ascends into heaven (Acts 1, 1-11); With Mary waiting for the coming of the Holy Spirit (Acts 1, 15-25); Jesus sends the Holy Spirit upon the disciples (Acts 2, 1-12)

33

Fruits of the tree

You, who come to this hillside, breathe in its air. Yes, open wide your heart, let the fragrance of the countryside fill your lungs. You are treading the ground where I had my roots. In the early morning, long before I splashed a little water on my face, I gently pushed back the shutter of my bedroom window and listened to the earth. God's good earth. Pulsating nature awakening. Sounds issuing forth from their silent bed to accompany the dawn. The hills putting on robes of light and the scent of the countryside. Beneath your feet, right where you are standing, is my land. My cradle – the soil, the tastes, the joys and pains. *Bosco*, the woods where trees find growth – I'm proud of you. A tree: sap and wood coming together; a marriage of soil and seasons. There is a museum right under your feet, a museum which tells of my roots, of the way of life of lowly people. Everyday objects, ordinary utensils. Tools that shape people and live in their language. Where you stand they've placed a memorial to my land. It's here that I grew up, pushing my roots farther and deeper. Little by little, the bark has hardened.

The sap has done its work, an unbroken flow between heaven and earth. The tree has grown tall. Bosco is now 'father'.
The bark is carved with so many young faces. That's why, at a stone's throw from where you are, they've now set up an anthropology museum which holds treasures from the five continents where I've sent my Salesian children. So many generous men and women have spread my branches to reach the children of Patagonia and Africa, whose pain they've shared and whose hopes they've made their own. Come and wonder at these stunning colours and exotic shapes. Come and be amazed at the tally of fruits in the thousands that this land has provided. *You know a tree by its fruits*, says the Gospel. Know that God has taken root in each one of us. Now it's for you to be courageous enough to bear fruit.

34

Visible in the distance, the village of Mondonio where Dominic Savio was born.

Dominic Savio

Dominic Savio came from the same area as Don Bosco and was taught by him at Valdocco in Turin. He died at fifteen. The Church has declared him to be the patron saint of young people

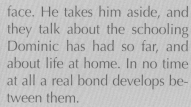

- *Dominic! Dominic! Wait for me! Your poor dad can't keep up with you!*
- *I'll run as far as the crossroad!*

It's the 2 October 1854, and since early morning Dominic has been restless. He has one thing only in mind: to meet Don Bosco at the Becchi – and he can't get there fast enough. His Dad is so slow!

Don Cagliero, his parish priest and former companion of Don Bosco at the seminary, has made all the necessary arrangements for this meeting.

- *Look, Dad, there's the Becchi!* Charles Savio put a gentle hand on his twelve-year-old son's shoulder.

- *I know, Dominic. I know. I often go that way to Castelnuovo.*

They make their way down towards the hamlet. 'Like father, like son' they say. Charles Savio has a forge. He's a hardy man of faith, and he and his wife Brigitte have made sure that their son is getting a good, solid education.

Don Bosco is on holiday with a group of youngsters from Turin, staying at his brother Joseph's house. It's there that they meet. The priest is delighted to see the joy and enthusiasm in Dominic's

face. He takes him aside, and they talk about the schooling Dominic has had so far, and about life at home. In no time at all a real bond develops between them.

- *Well, I think there's some good material in you!*
- *And what can be done with this material?* asks Dominic.
- *We can make a good garment and offer it to the Lord.*
- *So I'm the material, and you'll be the tailor. Will you take me to Turin, then?*

Don Bosco has enough experience of tailoring to know what Dominic is talking about. Dominic is the son of a seamstress; often he's seen his mother taking measurements to adjust a neighbour's clothes. They understand each other perfectly.

They both have the faith and trust in God to find common ground even at the spiritual level, and Don Bosco is quite amazed at the depth of faith he finds in this young boy. He quickly understands that the Lord is giving him a unique opportunity to nurture sanctity here.

Following a brief chat with the father, the whole matter is settled: Dominic will go to Turin, to study at Valdocco with a view to becoming a priest.

37

Chieri

- Hey! Bosco, are you coming? We're going into town!
Filipello, a school friend, is inviting John Bosco to have
a look around Cheri. John has just come here
to pursue his studies. He has left his native place for
the first time, and he's finding out what it's like to live
in a bustling town.
They are standing in front of the Town Hall, and before
long they'll be visiting some of the churches. Cheri
has much to offer. It boasts a theatre and two hospitals and two splendid piazzas that are the pride
of the town, both of them regularly
used for the market. In one you can
buy wine, fuel, fish and pottery;
in the other, cattle, hay and straw.
The smell of spices teases your
nostrils, and the bright colours
of billboards catch the eye.

- See you tomorrow for Sunday Mass at the Duomo.
That's the name they give to the church of Santa Maria
della Scala. There are many churches and shrines, but
the Duomo and the Church of St George are the only
two parish churches.
The two college friends rarely had a chance to get out
in the hills and sit quietly contemplating the town in
the light of the setting sun. To the eye it looked like a
place that had sprung up from the plain, tilting a little
towards the south. A small river followed the contours
of its surrounding walls, and a canal
powered its mill wheels, except in
the summer when it was dried up.
John Bosco was one of the poorer
pupils, who had to make great sacrifices
to pay for their lodgings, doing heavy
work in after-school hours.

A bright, lively mind

- Well, Vincent, how's your new student getting on?
- I must tell you that he's a real prodigy! And the other day there was quite a rumpus in the class because of him …

Don Valimberti couldn't believe his ears. Vincent Cima had a reputation for discipline that went far beyond the walls of the college.

- But it's true. Just imagine: this young fellow Bosco hadn't brought his Latin book; yet when I began putting questions to him, he opened a grammar book, and was able to give me the whole Latin text they had been given to study! What a memory he has! The whole class applauded wildly!
- Didn't I tell you? Remember, he began the year with Don Pugnetti and two months later he skipped a year and came to me. That's why I sent him to you for a test. He'll skip another year without any problem… But I've had to warn him. The rest are a lazy lot: they keep asking to copy his work, and he just can't say no.
- I'm inclined to think that he'll be a great asset there. For someone older and bigger than the rest of the class, it's never smooth going.
- But I've heard that on weekends he hangs around with others in piazzas!

Don Valimberti was not at all pleased by his colleague's harsh words. He had been outraged by an earlier disparaging remark made about young Bosco, this time in public:

- Either this fellow's a blundering nuisance, or he's a genius.
- I do know that he has started some sort of group of friends that they call 'The happy Club'. Nothing wrong in that!

For the time being, John Bosco was lodging with the widow Lucia Matta, in exchange for some domestic work and evening lessons for her son, and along with his long-time friend John Filipello, he was getting to know the town and its population of youngsters. Among them they found the whole gamut from vice to simple mischief, and mingling with them they were beginning to sort the wheat from the chaff. At that time in Chieri many students found life very grim, but fellows like Bosco had learned long ago how to face hardship.

The world out there

What's the use of slogging away day after day? I'm from the town. My dad can't hold down a job; my mum flits from one lousy job to another – what use to me is a fancy education, even if I stick with it? Teachers talk about things beyond me, or they just bore me. All my pals say the same. The school ignores us, and in any case, we don't need it. Get around a bit, and you'll be better off than with some diploma. Anyone who gets great marks is just a 'nerd'. Better to quit now before they throw us out. If we're not going to make it here, why stay shut up in these four walls that mean nothing? Outside, at least, in the street or the shopping arcades, there's life, activity, and people ….

I've dreamt that I would make it; see my secret plan come true. I've seen myself making furniture. I love the smell of wood. Whenever I skip school, I go into the carpentry shop near here. The boss knows me – how could he not! I watch him, notice his precise actions that produce these finely shaped objects. He runs his fingers over them gently to test the smooth finish. I would like to do something useful, to help people. But when you're a good-for-nothing – that's what my mother calls me when she reads my school reports – what use are dreams! When you just can't make it, you feel bad. It makes me bitter.

But there are some who do make it, like my pal Melchior. He hangs in, but I'm just a dropout.
I really know that won't get me anywhere. And it's not that I see myself as a loser, but I feel nothing goes right for me. Still, he has tried to help me. Melchior would love to see others making it too. OK! Back to work! I'll stop gazing out of the window. What was that next question I had to do? You never know…

A leader's exploits

I can't get to sleep! Is it the pain in my forearms and all up my legs, or is it just that I can't get over the fact that I won? John turns over in bed, struggling with all the thoughts and emotions running through his head. A few hours earlier he had beaten the local acrobat.

I beat him at running. OK! I beat him at jumping. OK! But I did beat him too at the top of the tree! When I got to the highest branch, I knew there was no farther to go. So I bent over, my weight on my hands, praying that I wouldn't break my bones (I did it for you, Lord! I did it to stop that phony from coming to disturb us every Sunday.) Then I curled into a ball, and as soon as my pals saw me like that, they guessed what I was going to do, and their shouts and cheers gave me the nerve to pull off the final feat. What if my mother had seen that! "He'll kill himself!" I felt the tree and its very sap steadying me. I stretched my legs high above the tree-top.

- Bosco is king! Three cheers for Bosco, our chief!
They went crazy with joy, these friends from the 'Happy Club'. Not one of them doubted that I would win.
One of them, Francis, had challenged the acrobat:
- If you lose, you leave.
John Bosco is in high spirits tonight. It's the triumph of the little cowherd from the Becchi. At seventeen,

he's riding high. How things can change! How he suffered when he first started school at Chieri – his classmates were two years younger, and he towered over them. But within a year he'd covered three years' work and moved on.
Now he's caught up.
It's all too much, all too much.
No wonder he can't sleep. He's the undisputed leader of his group. There's no one in Chieri who doesn't know John Bosco. Everybody wants to be his friend. More and more want to join the 'Happy Club'. Both teachers and parents know all about it, and all speak well of this happy group. No coarse language is ever heard, they share excellent reading matter and have lively discussions, and all is done for the Lord.
My God, I am so proud. Deliver me from these notions that make me forget your goodness.
As thoughts run through his mind, he brings them into a prayer and finally calms down.
If I'm to be a priest, I must talk these things over with my confessor.

His own man

John Bosco is a born leader. People listen to him, he has authority, and when he launches some project his enthusiasm is contagious. When he decides to start a group among school friends in Chieri, he has no problem gathering in a large number. But he's demanding; he doesn't want any half-measures. Young people have always loved to get together in their own place, to do their own thing away from adults. Often enough they don't know how best to spend their time, and they end up acting on impulse without considering the consequences.

John Bosco is a young man with a purpose. If he gets people together it's to do something, achieve something, have a useful objective, help someone. He's a positive leader. His qualities are ones that he has inherited from those few adults who meant something to him: his mother, Don Colosso, and one or other of his teachers. He's also following a dream that he won't give up on, so there's no time to waste or to see his group fritter away. And when he's convinced he has a just cause, he isn't afraid to take on anyone who would stand in his way. We sometimes complain about the number of young people who are drifters: they seem to be under-achievers who waste their energies in sterile pursuits. But maybe it is the way life is presented to them that destroys their initiative. Do we know how to give them responsibility and show that we can trust them? They are tomorrow's adults, and they need, now, to explore their ability to work and organise together responsibly. It's up to us to encourage them to be agents in their own life – to be their own person.

The river where John Bosco and the acrobat held a jumping contest

43

Studying the hard way

Chieri is asleep; silence reigns; the streets are empty. The last night owls have left the Pianta cafe. John Bosco locks up, tidies the billiard room and casts an eye over the counter. He climbs robot-like up the narrow stairs into a small space above the oven. In another two hours the bread will be baking. The day isn't over yet.

I got used to having little sleep when I was at home. I spend two thirds of the night reading a book by candlelight. I've no choice if I want to study. In any case, don't my friends have to do the same? It's only those from rich, noble families who don't have to make these sacrifices. In practice I read one book a day – Italian classics that Elias, the bookseller loans me for a penny. Like Elias, my best friend Jonas is also a Jew. Like me, he lost his father. Thanks to him Elias let me into the bookshop. I've noticed that he's interested in my religion and the prayers I say. When we talk we often get around to the question of faith.

Since Jews aren't allowed to work on a Saturday or even do any school work, John Bosco helps them by taking their classes that day, to avoid anyone making fun of them and humiliating them. He also lends a hand down the street with half a dozen youngsters who lodge with the veterinarian, Torta. Last year, when he was lodging for a second year with the widow Matta, he tutored her son John-Baptist, who was in fact six years his senior. With great tact and sensitivity he conducted the lessons. Now they've left Chieri, and John has found lodgings with friends of theirs who have recently opened a cafe. He's there now, doing a barman's hours.

It's a tough existence here with my boss, John Pianta. He gives me a bed and a bowl of soup each day. I'm often famished. A young boy, Joseph Blanchard, brings me fruit and chestnuts from his mother's shop. I try to forget I'm hungry, and I spend my free time with Jonas, playing the piano and singing. He has a very fine voice – but I often beat him at billiards!

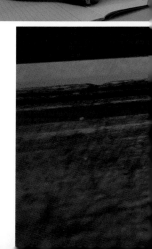

44

The small classroom in Capriglio,
where Don Bosco went to
school as a youngster

Padre nostro, che sei
ne' cieli, sia santificato
l tuo nome : venga il
o regno, sia fatta la
a volontà come in cie-
così in terra. Dacci
gi il nostro pane quo-
iano; e rimetti a noi i
tri debiti, come noi li
ettiamo ai nostri de-
ri ; e non c'indurre
ntazione, ma libe-
dal male. Così sia.

Bitter poverty

Each time he thinks about it, his eyes fill up. The young John Bosco puts his face in his hands and prays. It's the shame of the poor. Words are of no avail, only his body can tell the tally of the years: the twenty kilometres a day to school in Castelnuovo, his boots hanging round his neck, his eyes down to avoid the looks of passers-by. His back bent each morning as he goes down the cellar of the Pianta cafe to draw wine, and the tiring daily chores – all for four pence.

His bleary eyes at the end of the day, ravaged by tiredness and the smoke of the billiard players. His hands, blistered and bleeding at the top of the greasy pole in the Piazza Monta-fiat: it has taken him almost an hour to get up there, amid catcalls from the crowd; and now, with a twenty lire note between his teeth, John grabs a sausage and a neckerchief before sliding down again in the oil and grease, his legs bruised and scarred. At Moncucco, working for a whole year for a meagre fifteen lire! Begging from neighbours, his hand aching from knocking on doors, begging for money to pay his lodgings in Chieri. *It's a shame to see such a fine boy having to beg for money for his schooling, and not give him something!*

He has his fill of the snide remarks from hired labourers in the fields: *What use is that book? Do a decent job like us and the boss will pay you.* Yes, John Bosco knows the cost and the sacrifice to be able to study. He has learned to ignore the sweat and strain to pay for bed and board at the tailor shop in Castelnuovo. In his after-school work at the forge, he had to strain his muscles to keep a grip on the large tongs at the smithy, and not flinch as the heavy hammer blows came down. And when it came to sleeping, it was under a staircase, or in a barn, or now, above the oven where the bread is baked. When it comes to night prayer, he rests his head on his hands, speaks to God in the mystery of his lowly life, and the face of Christ, forever insulted, is imprinted on his weary palms.

Hamburger, chips and dream bubbles

William is no conqueror. He's one of those who just goes with the flow. Quiet at home, kept out of trouble at school, and now he's a young man who has trouble finding his place in a society that seems to be made only for conquerors, winners, influential people.

His CV is as blank as a frozen lake, just like his life. What he lacks is the will, the ambition, the passion to make progress. He'll never win a prize for top worker in the country.

He puts in his hours behind the counter at McDonald's, but he's not interested in the customers – they belong to a different world. His work is repetitive, it gives him no joy, no accomplishment, and when he gets home late at night, he takes the smell of the fat-frier into his room, with its one window that looks out on the wall opposite.

When anyone asks him what his work is, he invents impressive titles to hide from the awful reality of a life that he feels is slowing decaying. His bank account will never be in the black, because of the debts he keeps running up. He knows there are training programmes that would help him to get a qualification, find a job he would really like, and look to improve his life-style. But when he realises what it takes, the little dream bubbles that float around his head burst in an instant. For William there's no point in dreaming about a fine car, a girl who will fall in love with him, or a holiday in the sun. His horizon is no farther away than the door of the job centre. He goes there now and again. All he's looking for is some new job that's a bit less menial.

A formidable character

The street performer, poor fellow, doesn't always come off best. How can it be that a mere student can beat him, a professional? What's more, the whole challenge seemed to have been planned ahead.

- *This group of novices set it up, because they say my Sunday performance takes people away from the Jesuit lectures at St Anthony's church! What a laugh … except that it almost ruined me. As the stakes went up, I wagered all I had – 215 lire!* He repeats, yet again, the sad tale of his bad luck in Chieri. One of his friends tries to cheer him up:

- *But you're a terrific sprinter, you're famous for the long jump, and your balancing act with the hat on a stick is just magic! You're a star! And as for shinnying up a tree, no one can touch you!*

- *I know. It's just that this guy who took me on is no mere student. It cost me another 25 lire to settle the wager his pals bet on him.*

They said to me: this Bosco is no daddy's boy. He's from the Becchi, a peasant, a natural strong man. He was chasing animals from the age of four, and doing bodybuilding by loading hay carts. He worked at Savio's smithy as well. You should see his biceps!

- *He sounds more like a manual worker than a student.*

- *That's not true; they say lots of students do work to pay for their schooling. But there's nothing this one can't do. He learned wood-work, then tailoring, and just now he's a waiter in one of the cafes. So gifted as well! In the cafe he has everybody entertained with stories and poems, and gets them all singing. He's really good at music….*

- *Well, I think with a chap like that, you should get him on your side.*

- *Not a hope! You haven't heard it all yet. The only thought in his head is to become a priest! A character like that will surely go places.*

Hands made to create

The hand is a brilliant creation; possibly the most wonderful of God's gifts. When you look closely, it seems so ordinary. It isn't even a thing of beauty. And yet what a precision instrument it is! Just a collection of skin, flesh, bones, tendons and nerves, and yet it moves, opens and closes, gives and receives. At times its touch is gentle, at other times firm and strong.

With your hand you can strike and hurt, tear and break. Your hand can become a fist, closed and used like a weapon. But it can also express feelings: the sticky palm of the fearful one, the trembling hand of the emotional one, the reassuring hand of one who loves and uplifts.

When the hand takes up a tool, it takes on a new beauty. It acquires a new, creative power. With a tailor's needle and scissors, a carpenter's plane, a blacksmith's hammer, it has a new dimension. Its precise actions bring to birth a new creation, something that will be of use, bring comfort and perhaps joy to the one who will receive it.

One who has learned the beauty of these actions can also teach them to others, pass on the skill he has acquired. In this gift of oneself, life is given and received. What lies at the heart of every apprenticeship is that, in creating something new, we discover our true self.

49

The loneliness of decision-making

Bosco the acrobat. Bosco the life and soul of the party. The one who can always cheer you up and put a smile on your face. The friend who will do anything for you, from mending your clothes to going over a lesson.

Oh, they make me smile! If only they knew what's gripping my heart! If only there were someone who knew me well and was perceptive enough to see beyond appearances! If I only had a true friend to understand me and advise me! Someone courageous enough to stay close to me in my searching, wise enough to help me name what's hurting me, and be a shoulder to lean on when I feel deeply troubled. But I'm on my own. Horribly alone.

Dark thoughts weigh me down and create doubts. Questions I can't even put words to; more like fleeting ghosts. Worries attack me like an invisible enemy. There's no let-up. They destroy my peace of mind and rob me of my sleep. Even my dreams torment me, and I can't explain them. In them, I see strange figures of Franciscan friars running in all directions, just when I'm on the point of joining them. Will I not become a friar, after all?

My mother came over to Chieri yesterday, and she told me I don't owe her anything; she's not counting on me to look after her in her later years, and I must simply do the will of God. And then there's Don Dassano, parish priest of Castelnuovo, who talks quite openly about the doubts I shared with him! Yes, I'm alone, horribly alone, walled in by worries. Even my confessor won't give me any lead; on principle, because he says he mustn't influence my free choice. But what if it's true? What if he doesn't believe in my vocation to the priesthood, and he doesn't dare tell me, for fear of damaging my hopes and ambitions and wounding my pride? Everything in me is confused and fiercely complicated.

John's old boss, the blacksmith, his face bathed in sweat, pauses between blows on the anvil, and tells him calmly and confidently:

- Gianni! Go to Don Cafasso in Turin and ask his advice. He's young and from Castelnuovo. Everybody around here thinks highly of him.

- Thanks, Mr Savio.

I can't tell him how much he's just like a father to me – he would just laugh at the thought.

You are calling me

The earth spins alone,
What more could I do?
All was going well for me,
But you came by ....
Why are you calling me?
Why are you disturbing me?
I was doing so well.
Pass me by!

I had it all worked out,
My plans, my friends.
Till then, all went well,
But what are you doing here?
Why are you calling me?
Why are you disturbing me?
I was doing so well.
Pass me by!

You promise happiness,
But I feel afraid.
I'm really no better than the rest,
Better look elsewhere.
Why are you calling me?
Why are you disturbing me?
I was doing so well.
Pass me by!

An enriching friendship

- *You're very talented, John! Who taught you to be so skilful at woodwork?* Louis Comollo carefully picks up John's writing case, feeling the wood, so smoothly and precisely assembled and finished.
- *I learned to use a plane and a wood chisel when I was lodging in St George Street. I used to go a carpenter's shop near St William Square, to make money for my school fees, and nowadays I do small jobs for myself.*

Louis, who joined the seminary in October 1836, is his best friend, and John appreciates his compliments. Although Louis is two years younger, John finds his company very congenial.
- *You see, says Louis, we have to let the Lord do his work on us, just as the carpenter does his work.*
- *You're right. Look at my namesake, John Bosco from Rivalta. He often says, "I'm the 'medlar' Bosco". Medlar is a hardwood.*
And I say, "I'm the 'willow' Bosco", because willow is a softwood, and easy to work.
- *True ... but there's still some work to be done! Remember how often you lose you temper!*

- *I know you're right, Louis. But I am trying more and more to follow your advice.*
- *I can see that you're putting in a lot of effort to discipline yourself. The more time we can give to prayer, the more the Lord will give us the graces we need.*

As they move on, Louis Comollo is John's close friend, willing to urge and prod him spiritually, in season and out of season. John admires him, almost envies him for his prayerfulness and his serene trust in God. This is not surprising, because for John the first months of seminary life are a real test and a big sacrifice. He needs a worthwhile antidote. At recreation times he unwinds with lively card games. He isn't the best of players, but he has a knack of almost always winning! Often enough, even during work and prayer, his mind is on cards! In Louis, with his courtesy and warm friendship, John sees an example of something he can't yet acquire on his own. Here John Bosco, the future master of pedagogy, is learning the value and the efficacy of a gentle, kindly presence.

What salvation do I need?

Salvation and the hereafter were worrisome preoccupations of the era. Don Bosco and Louis Comollo made an agreement: "Whoever dies first will send the other one news from beyond". In fact, after the death of Louis Comollo, whom he survived by twenty-two years, Don Bosco recounted that he had received a sign from him.

They say that Christ came to save humanity: from whom? from what? What danger threatens us? Granted, in the Gospel we see that he saves certain ones from a disease, or some wretched situation, others from some dependency, or oppression, or even death itself. He does seem to be very concerned about the condition people find themselves in, especially the most vulnerable and despised.

They say also that his passion, death and resurrection took place to offer us salvation. But what salvation do I need? I organise my life is such a way as to avoid any immediate dangers, and as for the ones that can't be foreseen, who can save me from them? It's a matter of luck.

I do admit that there are tendencies in me that I don't really control, and sometimes they get the upper hand. There's a degree of aggression, and perhaps a slight attraction for what I know is forbidden and not morally acceptable. As for other people's misfortune, and my being top dog, I have to admit that's sometimes the way I want it, and I take pleasure in it. But then, I've no sooner admitted it than I suppress the thought and deny it happened. Such a thing can't come from me! That's not the real me!

When I feel outraged by acts of violence and injustice committed by others, I have a niggling suspicion that what motivated them is probably lurking in me too. I just have to make sure I never give vent to those dark forces that come from the depths of our human nature, and which I admit do scare me a little when I feel them rising up in spite of me.

Maybe, after all, I too need a saviour: someone who will free me from these negative urges that are in me. I do want this freedom, but I need some work done on me. Christ offers to help me in this work. When that happens, he really is my saviour, making me free to give expression in myself to all that is good and beautiful. It's then that I discover the image of the Father in me.

53

Cut off from the outside world

The huge seminary building at Chieri protects its occupants as an oyster jealously guards its pearl. The church of St Philip stands between Via Maestra and a former monastery, which in 1828 had been handed over to the Archdiocese of Turin by royal decree, for the education of future priests. The rector, Don Sebastian Mottura, must be delighted that the church, built earlier by monks, forms an effective spiritual air cushion, insulating the seminary from the incessant hustle and bustle of the street. Isn't it his intention, after all, to withdraw his students from the world outside, and especially from the sound wave rolling past all day long, carrying the frenzied, money-minded preoccupations of the business world? The house of God, therefore, filters out very nicely all the extraneous street noise, giving the devotional life its rightful place. Far from the polluted air of worldly concerns, six conscientious clerics are engaged in teaching all the virtues and duties needed by seminarians. *It is necessary that these young men become like the One they represent. With the power invested in them by God, they must, as priests, be able to proclaim his law to the people, in such a way that their congregation will revere not mere men, but Jesus himself who speaks through them.* The assignment is clear and precise. While this may stimulate the team of lecturers, it is not guaranteed to give them peace of mind, given the complexity of the task. At 4.30 a.m. everybody is up. They dress in silence and then recite the Angelus. Half an hour later the chapel resounds with their morning prayers. Next, a member of staff reads the text set for meditation. Then it is time for Mass, followed by an hour of study in silence. The rhythm of the day is fixed. Rules are clear and unchangeable. Before long the students happily accept the tinkle of a bell as a command to be obeyed. This seminary life is seen as laying a solid foundation for the formation of exemplary, docile pastors needed to guide the faithful through the temptations and pitfalls of life. Don Mottura knows this full well. Only the conviction that he is supported by Divine Providence allows him to look forward to a smooth start to the year.

A sun-dial, the only original feature of the severe seminary of Chieri. It is no longer there, but it was restored and relocated.

56

Time

It flows as if in a huge egg-timer.
The clock towers sound out its rhythm.
Fortunately, it can't be stopped
On its slow march to eternity.
Time!

Sophisticated instruments measure it,
Astronomical clocks fix it
In history and in space.
Talking clocks tell it precisely.
Time!

Others capture the circling arc
Of a sunbeam projecting
Across numbers, with the shadow of a needle.
Sundials, masterpieces
Of time.

Time slips like sand through the fingers.
No longer do we have time to take our time.
There's nostalgia for the good old times,
And fear of bad times to come.
And yet…

There is a time for everything.
A time to search and a time to find.
A time to reflect, a time to rest.
A time to consider, a time to act.
A time for rest, a time to see and be involved.
A time for silence, a time to speak.
A time to sow, a time to reap.
A time to love, a time to forgive.
A time to doubt, a time to hope.
A time to suffer, a time to die.

All the special times mark the year.
There is a time to pray, and a prayer for time!

57

Turin

The leaden, grey sky droops over the city, spitting out a filthy drizzle. A dark, grimy mist hovers over the rooftops, forming ghostly shapes. Little chimneysweeps, shivering and soot-spotted, are hard at their hazardous work. This is a far cry from the green hills of years past! These youngsters have come with their parents, leaving behind the crippling poverty of peasant life, and hoping to find an Eldorado in the city. Wherever you go in Turin, theirs are the little hands hoping to earn a few pence: street vendors, shoe-shiners, errand boys, chimneysweeps, stable lads, child labourers. These are the children of the Industrial Revolution, which began in England and is now turning European cities upside down. The invention of the steam engine has given birth to massive mechanisation, which in turn has spawned factories and their workers. Progress has been prolific, but *a small number of very rich men have been able to lay upon the teeming masses of the labouring poor a yoke little better than that of slavery itself.**

When Don Bosco makes his way through the streets of Turin in 1841, he finds a city undergoing a radical transformation. Between 1838 and 1848, the population has risen from 117,000 to 137,000 – an increase of 17%. In those ten years, 7,000 families have been crammed into 700 newly built houses. Migration peaked in 1849-1850 with between 50,000 and 100,000 immigrants.

Lack of suitable dwellings often forces working-class people to huddle together in a single room which has to serve as bedroom, kitchen, and sometimes even workshop. Because of this, children often end up on the streets, exposed to *every kind of danger and temptation*. These are the youngsters Don Bosco discovers. It's all too clear to anyone passing through the city that there's a crying need for schools, leisure facilities, training programmes, and to a priest like Don Bosco, for religious education.

He's ready to put his shoulder to the task. He won't be the only one, but he will put his own personal stamp on what he does.

*Encyclical 'Rerum Novarum', 15 May 1891

Priest, of the people, for the people

Excitement is high in Turin on Saturday, 5 June 1841. What's going on in the minds of those twenty-six deacons shortly to be ordained priests? Right now each one is conscious of the huge step he's about to take. The bishop, Louis Fransoni, accompanied by forty-two priests, will ordain these young men in the church of the Immaculate Conception.

I have only one wish: that I should be a worthy priest of our Lord, Jesus Christ, faithful to his mission, and able to save the souls of those entrusted to me. John Bosco is quite overcome by the emotion and intensity of the previous few days – the last week of a long story that began so humbly at the Becchi; a week of spiritual exercises and prayer, to become a new man in Christ. With all the help, encouragement and advice he has received, any obstacles, doubts or mistakes have been well and truly laid to rest.

Yesterday at Alfiano, I had just given my first sermon as a priest, and Don Pelato, the parish priest, took my arm and gave me the following valuable piece of advice.

- John, you'll have to give up that florid, literary style of language. Speak in the local dialect, or, if you prefer, in Italian, but in a popular style. I repeat, a popular style. Instead of long explanations, give examples. Make simple, practical comparisons. Remember that people don't listen a great deal, and you have to explain the truths of the faith in the simplest way possible.

What a wet blanket that was! There was I, so proud of my homily. I, who wanted to show these people what a fine preacher I was! I shall never be able to thank that man enough for having stubbed out my pride and all my pretensions. I'm quite sure that Don Bosco will be a priest of the people and for the people. The little peasant from the Becchi will be a humble pastor for men and women who have to struggle through all the pitfalls of life. Who can understand the fears of ordinary people better than one of their own? When I was young, I learned to walk across a rope, tied between two trees. Now I'll make the most of all those balancing skills to help people cross from one riverbank of life to another. May the Blessed Virgin watch over and protect me!

To begin to say Mass is to begin to suffer.

It's nice to be able to sit down! What a day we've had! For some people, used to the simple, good-hearted ways of country life, it was likely to go to their head! But the humble peasant woman from the Becchi knew how to keep a cool head. She had lived long enough not to be bowled over by compliments and flattery. It was 'Congratulations!' from this one and 'I'm so pleased for you!', from this other, and on it went. And all those strangers, usually so distant, and those priests who normally kept to themselves, coming to congratulate her.

Margaret Bosco, aged 53, has just lived through a most extraordinary day. It's the Feast of Corpus Christi, and her son, John, has just celebrated his first Mass in his native place. This was a Solemn High Mass, followed by the procession of the Blessed Sacrament, which John also led, carrying the monstrance in the usual way beneath the canopy. A banquet had been organised, to which clergy and local dignitaries were invited. This mother can see just how much her son is esteemed and loved. John is the hero of the day, and everyone wants to be his friend. How many times the tale about the little tightrope walker has been told, with two or three versions at least, each one milking the story for best effect. Singing praises and celebrating have their place, but John's mother keeps a down-to-earth sense of reality about her children. In the still of the evening, she has a few quiet words of advice for her son: *John, now that you are a priest, you are much closer to Jesus. I haven't read books as you have, but remember that to begin to say Mass is to begin to suffer. You won't realise it right away, but little by little you'll see that your mother was right. From now on, think only of the salvation of souls, and don't worry about me.*

Training for life

The stench hits you as soon as you go through the main door. Wild howls are yelled out from every floor, and piercing, high-pitched sounds that can only come from very young throats. Obscenities and blasphemies fill the air. This is a prison, but what sort of humanity is here that screams out its venomous hatred? The young priest, Don Bosco, is racked with revulsion. Don Cafasso has advised him to come here for his pastoral work, and now he's a weekly visitor. On his rounds he also calls at the hospital known as the 'little house' of Divine Providence, run by Canon Cottolengo, who cares for those who are abandoned or considered incurable, ravaged either in body or in mind. Other priests, fellow students of Don Bosco, go with him to visit poor families crammed into new suburbs. In the past, he has only known the poverty in the countryside, but now he is discovering the sombre reality of the poverty that goes with the progress of the industrial revolution. The theologian Don Guala,

with the help of Don Cafasso, had opened an Ecclesiastical Institute in a former monastery near the church of St Francis of Assisi. Its purpose was the training of forty-five young priests who would play leading roles in the Church's mission in the society of their day. Don Guala would give a conference each morning, and Don Cafasso in the evening, and much of the rest of the day would be spent either in the city or in the suburbs visiting places of work. Gangs of young people would wander through the streets and along the banks of the river Po, especially on Sundays. Scared, but defiant, they would give a wide berth to anyone who tried to come near them. For them, in this urban jungle, where each one tried to find a small place in the sun, it was a fight for survival. Don Bosco grasped the magnitude of this human disaster, which made him think back to the wild animals in his childhood dream. At all cost, he had to find young apostles to go right to the heart of this world of the young.

8-70

63

Street children

Don Bosco hunting for souls

If you want a breath of fresh air, you'd better go out early morning, because once the sun is up, your nostrils are filled with a cocktail of dusty smells. The whole countryside of Piedmont spreads out its rich, attractive produce on the Turin pavements. At Porta Palazzo (now known as Piazza della Republica) you can buy anything you want. It's the most popular market in the city; just fifteen minutes walk from Valdocco. Amid this kaleidoscope of warm colours, rough accents and infectious laughter, the women settle behind their abundant stalls, while husbands and children are unloading, carrying, piling up, weighing and checking. Always on the move to please the customer; a busyness that suggests good business. The mother's trained eye never leaves her stall: every least article for sale has to be protected from roving rascals. These little rogues are all around, bold as brass, darting between legs, spying the chance of a quick snatch for something to appease their hunger. You'd feel sorry for these poor wretches, but the vendors know that if they give way to one, they'll be opening the floodgates for a host of others. It's only when they are packing up that they pretend to overlook a few fruits or vegetables to satisfy these starving stomachs, but in the meantime it's strict business as usual. Amid the moving masses of people, and the pervasive smells, each one sings the praises of his own produce. Prices are chalked up – the cheapest on the market, of course! – to coax shoppers into buying. Don Bosco loves to come here and connect with his roots again. He spots the people he knows, who can give him news from his home place, just twenty kilometres from Turin, where he spent his youth. The regulars know him well. He's the priest who gathers these youngsters together. He even goes looking for them on the various work sites. He's the conscience of the city. He doesn't buy anything, because he hasn't the money, and if he does ask for a few fruits, they are reluctant to charge him. Won't he be taking them straight away to the youngsters by the fountain? That's where Don Bosco goes *looking for souls*. Among the chaff of those who sneer at him, he can spot the good grain to take to his Oratory. *Poor priest*, says one old man. *Just look how these good-for-nothings make fun of him! I couldn't care less about them. It isn't apples they need!* But a look from the priest quiets him. It seems to say: *Leave them alone. They're my friends.*

At rock bottom

Jimmy is 17. He quit school last year and now spends his time walking the streets. For him school is just head-bashing. He wants to prove to his parents that he can achieve something – find work and earn money. He's soon disenchanted. What looked like freedom has become a nightmare. He trawls the agencies, but his situation gets worse. This is his day: gets up between 1 and 2 o'clock in the afternoon; eats whatever is left in the fridge. Next he joins his pals and spends most of the day sitting in stairwells. Back home, he nibbles a bit more, listens to music in his room, and finally turns in around 3 to 4 in the morning.

Everything is getting worse: relationships, job experience, and lapse into gutter language. He meets Chris, a peripatetic teacher, but nothing changes, though his time keeping does improve a little. He's inclined to let events dictate. An appointment for a job is ignored if something more interesting crops up. Where is that real freedom he dreamt of?

He feels he's being sidelined. He regularly gets into a sweat – bad for city life. It's just his luck. He can do nothing about it. How can he bounce back? He sees that Chris is just letting him sweat it out. What use are these so-called 'educators'? But in a chat with him, he finds that the man hasn't written him off, and he understands the hell he's been going through. Jimmy is at rock bottom, but he does want to climb back up. The man can see this and offers him a chance to spend a while on a mountain project, doing voluntary work. He agrees. The experience helps him to surface again and regain his confidence.

Back in the city, Chris suggests that he join a re-entry programme that will provide a suitable, progressive work plan and help him to get his bearings. From then on, everything will depend on Jimmy. His future is in his own hands.

A decisive meeting

- *Pardon me saying this, Father! But if you carry on encouraging boys like that good-for-nothing, I can't think where we'll all end up!*

It's the sacristy of the Church of St Francis of Assisi. The young priest has a smile on his face as he turns to the sacristan.

- *Look, I know you have very high standards, and …*
- *In that case, you should realise that this kind of youngster only spells trouble. Just take you eyes off him for a second, and ….*
- *But didn't you see, he was fine when he was with me?*
- *With you, Father, yes, with you! But you are not always around, and when he comes back, who's going to take responsibility for him?*
- *That's just the point – I've asked him to come back next Sunday.*
- *What! With all due respect, who's given permission for that?*
- *Look. This young fellow's name is Bartholomew Garelli. He's not a good-for-nothing, as you say, he's simply an orphan from Asti, and he's here looking for work. We must look out for young people like him.*
- *Look out for them! I tell you, Father, I can bring a whole horde of them as soon as you like!*

Don Bosco understands the sacristan's attitude. He still hasn't taken in what happened earlier. He had chased the youngster from the sacristy, and the young priest, who was preparing to celebrate Mass, told him to go and fetch the boy back. Don Bosco will not allow the poor lad to be treated like that. Even though he is a teenager, he is no villain. Don Bosco spent some time with him, ending with a prayer and the sign of the Cross.

- *You know, Joseph, ever since I came to Turin, not a day goes by when I don't come across youngsters like him, either on the streets or in the prison. But this one actually came here. Actually came into God's house!*
- *Uh … into the sacristy, you mean! And I wonder what he was really looking for!*
- *What do you think? A little warmth, of course …. not just from the freezing cold outside, but a little human warmth. Don't you understand?*
- *Oh, I know you, Don Bosco. Your kindness will be your undoing. Look: it's the 8 December*, there's a Mass every hour at each altar until 11 o'clock. Between youngsters hanging around and priests queuing up to say Mass, I don't know which way to turn!*
- *I can see that, but I have a feeling that with this lad Bartholomew, we'll really get somewhere. He's promised to come back for some instruction, and, with other boys he knows, we'll start an Oratory.**
- *An Oratory! Oh, you have my sympathy!* Don Bosco isn't the first idealist Joseph Comotti has come across. *Never mind, he thinks. He'll learn, just like heaps of others!*

**8th December 1841: Feast of the Immaculate Conception.*
**Oratory: youth centre.*

66

St Francis of Assisi

Surprised by the sound of young voices, the priest rushes to his window and looks out. It's Sunday, and Don Bosco, with official approval, has come to spend the afternoon with a group of youngsters in the courtyard of the Convitto*. That spells the end of that priest's siesta! How many are there this time? At least eighty. Already, for several months Don Bosco has been doing this, bringing young apprentices – stone-cutters, masons, pavers – or just day-labourers he finds in the various work-sites he visits in the course of a week. Some have only recently been released from prison and are a potential risk. Without his siesta, the priest is not best pleased, but also not unsympathetic. In the early days, when the group numbered about twenty, it was enough to set foot in the cloister, and the noise level would come down to a respectful silence. Don Bosco would give him an apologetic smile, and he would continue on his way to the church of St Francis of Assisi. But today there are so many of them, and they are so rowdy! Other well-meaning clerics pass through. Some offer holy pictures, rosaries or medals, though Don Bosco drops hints that he would prefer clothes, shoes or food, and even help to find work placements with some trustworthy employers. Don Bosco does try to take them on outings – he's fully aware that this courtyard is much too small, and the college isn't the ideal setting for this kind of apostolate – and he would dearly love to find an alternative so as to avoid causing a disturbance. It's enough to put anyone's nerves on edge with the racket they make! As the priest reaches the foot of the stairs and prepares to step out into the cloister, the sudden silence shocks him. The youngster's eyes are all on Don Bosco as he makes announcements.

Catching sight of the priest, Don Bosco says to them: And for confessions today, since there are so many of you, I can see that another priest has come to join us!

*The Convitto - a training college for young priests.

A period of effervescence

In the mid 19th century, Italy as we know it did not exist. There was just a mosaic of states, kingdoms and duchies in a loosely linked network of alliances or dependencies. Beneath it all there was something brewing which would explode in the revolution of 1848. The 'liberals' wanted to overturn the monarchy. The 'nationalists' wanted to break away from all submission to French and Austrian rule. Between the factions there was no common ground: for some the goal was the unification of Italy, for others a type of federation. In the midst of all that, the question of the Papal States remained unresolved, since the Church still exercised much political clout. On all fronts there were many challenges to face.

Add to that the economic crisis brought about by the industrial revolution which was changing the whole social fabric. Poverty was overwhelming the countryside, while towns were becoming an amorphous mass of people lacking clear, organised structures, where the most deprived had no legal protection. What had began as seasonal migrations to the towns became the constant norm. Chaotic shantytowns sprouted up. There were no schools. Basic human and Christian formation was non-existent. For many, it was purely a question of survival. As a result, on all non-working days, crowds of young workers and apprentices would hang around the streets and public squares, a situation leading to all sorts of disorders. This caused great concern to churchmen and statesmen alike, as they witnessed the social, moral and religious consequences, but they were at a loss to know how to address them. Sporadic attempts were made – literacy programmes, vocational training, and social initiatives – but all too little. A basic education for every child was needed, but inevitably, launching such a huge programme at a time of political instability, and with a host of other priorities, was fraught with problems.

Kingdom of Piedmont and Sardinia

Lucca

Duchies of Modena and Parma

Grand Duchy of Tuscany

68

Kingdom of Venice-Lombardy

The artisans of Italian unification:
Victor Emmanuel II,
Cavour and Garibaldi

Kingdom of the Two Sicilies

Papal States

The politics of the 'Our Father'

The Gospel figure that inspired Don Bosco's whole life was that of the Good Shepherd, who takes care of each one in every aspect of life. Thus, while proclaiming the gospel to young people, he also involved himself in vast social work, since the causes of deprivation, unemployment and lack of education were to be found in the disorganised society of the day. For that reason he didn't hesitate to make regular calls on the Piedmontese minister Urban Rattazzi. But for all that, he was his own man, freely speaking his mind and taking his own initiatives. As he would say, his only agenda was *'the politics of the Our Father'*.

Your kingdom come. A kingdom of love, justice, peace, and equity. For that Don Bosco would use every means possible – door-to-door begging for help, meetings to persuade authorities, cutting through red tape, minimising obstacles, stone-walling refusals, and clearing up wrong-headed ideas about him.

Your will be done. Don Bosco had a disciple's ear for the inspirations of the Lord who had given him his mission of apostle to the young. He could resist the injunctions of Bishop Gastaldi, the pressures of those who opposed him, and the threats of his detractors, but he remained the humble servant of Christ and of his representative, the pope.

Give us our daily bread. Don Bosco gave food and shelter to young people deprived of home life and affection. If some vital need arose, he faced it squarely. He earned his good name because he worked 'for the well-being of people'.

Lead us not into temptation. The politics of the Our Father required Don Bosco to keep a cool head – a sense of balance, like the young tightrope-walker he used to be. He knew what he was aiming for, and looked straight ahead so as not to lose sight of it; allowed nothing to distract him or put him off balance, since that spelled disaster. So many young people depended on him that he needed to be a realist. His sole ambition was to make them into mature people grounded in their faith and caring of others, happy in this life and in the life to come.

69

A crazy idea!

Don Bosco saw in every human being a heart that yearns to love and to be loved. That meant also every young person, even one who had committed the worst of crimes. Through Don Cafasso he had discovered first-hand the misery of hundreds of youngsters huddled together in prison.

In 1845 a new prison was built in Turin, known as the *Generala*, and Don Bosco became a regular visitor there. It held three hundred prisoners – among them many young people – in close confinement. Putting his trust in God, and in the young people themselves, he took the brave step of teaching them the faith and even doing a Lenten retreat. One day, seeing that he had built up a good bond of trust with the young prisoners, a seemingly crazy idea occurred to him: *Suppose I took them all on an outing. Just for a few hours, to let them breathe some fresh air, relax in the country and enjoy a taste of freedom!* It was a daring venture, so the prison governor sent him to the minister Ratazzi for authorisation. Don Bosco gave his word of honour: every single prisoner would be back for the roll call!

Don Bosco pulled it off. It was a day to remember. They walked, laughed and sang, and had a great picnic. In short, they had a whale of a time. They had made a double promise to Don Bosco: *We'll behave well, and we'll all come back.* They kept their word. Much to the surprise of the governor, not a single one failed to return – proof, if needed, that Don Bosco had been right to trust the youngsters and take them at their word.

Free at last …

It might seem paradoxical, but I feel free in my six-square-metre cell. Since I met Francis, the prison chaplain, my life has turned 180 degrees. Through him I've discovered the Bible. Since I had nothing to do, I began to read it and found I was in for some surprises. I do admit there are some stories that are hard to get my head round, like Jesus walking on water and raising his friend Lazarus from the dead after weeping over him. That's really beautiful. But the best of all is when he died on the cross. There were two criminals alongside him, and he promised one that he would be with him in paradise. That really blew my mind! I began to feel deep down my own need to be saved, and that only Jesus could do that. Me, the super gangster of a thousand and one escapades! I'd done it all. Now, I was asking the Lord to remember me. I'd hit rock bottom. Now I felt he was reaching out his hand to raise me up.

Since then, the silence of my cell doesn't feel heavy any more. I'm re-reading the story of my life and trying to understand where it went wrong. When Francis comes, he helps me to put my finger on it and see more clearly. I used to feel that my life was hurtling along at a hundred miles an hour. I didn't have time to really live. I was sinking beneath all my cravings …. I just lost it and fell into a deep hole. Thanks to the chats I'm having with Francis, I'm now seeing life so differently – real life! No longer a life where I push others down so as to come out on top, but one where we are all brothers. Through the words of Francis, and God's own words, I'm surfacing again, and finding an inner freedom. I still need more time to think about my future, but I've regained my self-confidence and found a sense of my own dignity before God.

A dynamic and generous woman

The Marchioness of Barolo, formerly Juliette de Colbert, was a married woman and a vivacious character whose life was totally dedicated to the poor. Though of French origin, she acquired great renown in Turin society. Widowed and childless at fifty-three, she would devote herself and her fortune to improving the quality of life of young women. Her first project was for women prisoners, then the creation of orphanages and hostels for young working girls. She then opened a refuge for prostitutes looking for a better way of life. She was even planning to build a hospital.

It was at this stage of her work that she first met Don Bosco. Another Turin priest, Don Borel, had suggested to the Marchioness that she should engage Don Bosco as spiritual director for her young women of the Refuge, in return for a stipend and living quarters. Don Bosco's main preoccupation was, of course, the continuation of his work for street children, though this arrangement did provide him with a playground, and his room gave him a place for Mass and confessions for his boys. However, this mutual agreement lasted only for a short while and finally collapsed over a misunderstanding, mainly due to the clash of two strong personalities. Don Bosco had secretly hoped to make use of part of the new building for his youngsters, whilst the Marchioness wanted Don Bosco to give his undivided commitment to her girls. For her, putting up with a noisy, turbulent crowd of boys was asking too much; and in any case, the inevitable contact between the two groups was less than desirable. The final separation was quite amicable however, and the Marchioness continued discretely supporting Don Bosco's work.

Aside from this brief episode, it has to be said that the Marchioness of Barolo was an outstanding woman, who displayed great energy and generosity. To the end of her life she remained faithful to the ideal she had set herself: in witness to her Christian faith, to give herself and all her resources in the service of the neediest young women.

Commitment to the little people

When Don Bosco reaches out to God's little ones, he doesn't come among them as a saviour. He is not some great hero coming to change everything and solve all the problems, as people often, and quite wrongly, talk about him.

He does have some very clear convictions which will shape his outlook and his line of action.

In the first place, the conviction that he has been sent by God : his commitment is a response to a mission he has received. He does nothing in his own name. His childhood dream has mapped out his involvement: who he is sent to, what his goal is, and how he must operate. He is at the service of this God-given task.

That explains why his presence among the most marginalised children is marked by assurance and respect. He can accept the tentative beginnings, the forced displacements, the rebuffs and rejections, whether from adults or the young people themselves.

When, like Don Bosco, you are at the service of an enterprise, you don't look for immediate results, come what may. You know that the twists and turns of events, and even the setbacks, are a prelude to further openings. Education is sometimes more productive only when time seems to drag its feet. Germination needs the winter, the cold and even the frost. That's how it is with Don Bosco's Oratory. It needs its passing phases, its temporary roots before it can begin to spread all its branches.

The greatest secret of Don Bosco, without any doubt, is his ability to make his young people his best partners. *Without you, I can do nothing* , he would say to them. These little people, the ones no one cares about, become the pillars of a great enterprise built on the Providence of God. They are his fellow builders, organisers, founders.

73

An area in turmoil

The police are puzzled. They've been put on the alert regarding these two priests. One of them is Don Bosco, organiser and linchpin of the whole movement. The other, an older priest, is the theologian Don Borel, who officially represents and administers the system. But what are they accused of? They've been under close surveillance now for several weeks, and nothing has come to light that could lead to an arrest. There's even been talk of a revolutionary movement. Granted, the police have had to issue warnings to one or two mindless individuals – some of them only speak in dialect – but nothing serious. All these priests do is teach catechism, hear confessions and sing hymns! The youngsters love them. Recently they were joined by a number of students – probably agitators, you might think. Nothing of the sort. They've come to lend a hand with literacy or catechism lessons, and in return Don Bosco helps them with their own studies. Superintendent Manzoni said his own son could do with a bit of help! As for drawing up an official report, that really is a headache. The number of youngsters involved? That's changing all the time, and going up. How can you count a group like this? Based on police experience, they reckon about three hundred just now. In any case, they never seem to gather in the same place. Rumour has it that they started in the grounds of the Marchioness Barolo. They say the whole area was in turmoil, with boys running around in the streets while the priests were in their rooms. Later they were seen at the cemetery chapel of St Peter in Chains, but local bylaws put an end to that. People were accusing them of profaning a sacred place. When they regrouped by the 'Mulini' flour mills, the police resumed their surveillance. The police chief, Marquis Michael de Cavour, received complaints from the secretary of the millers. The official deposition spoke of: *A hotbed of immorality. Disturbances and rowdyism every Sunday. Provocative taunts. Unlawful behaviour. Suspicious and possibly dangerous gangs.* Following a careful enquiry on our part, we found nothing more than a scratch mark on a wall! At this point in time, they are gathering by the Moretta house, between a field belonging to the Filippi brothers and a place owned by Francis Pinardi. The three policemen we sent to investigate find everything in order, and would willingly take off their uniforms and join in the games!

74

Valdocco outside-the-walls

There's our Valdocco, says Paul to one of his pals. It's Wednesday afternoon, and they are waiting as usual for the team leaders from this youth centre that takes its name from Don Bosco's first foundation. Other youngsters soon join them as numbers rise to about fifty. In no time, all the facilities are set up. There's a football pitch, a variety of games, a painting room for budding artists, a reading area well supplied with magazines and books – so many activities to help young people both to develop their potential and to acquire a team spirit.

In a world where a young person is often left to his or her own devices, and where the law of the strongest rules, taking part in well-regulated team activities provides an excellent learning experience for life in society. If a child is pulled aside following a show of violence, he is made to reflect on his wrong behaviour. Being taken aside is not a final exclusion, but a necessary moment to be made aware of the seriousness of what was done, and the consequences of that for the rest of the team. The educator uses this brief chat to affirm the youngster's much greater personal value compared with the misguided behaviour.

From week to week, youngsters and leaders get to know each other, a bond of trust is built up, and further links are made with parents.

This *Valdocco outside the walls* provides a bridge-building space for parents and children in a convivial environment, and as a consequence of sharing this common ground, the child's progress at school can benefit, while parents become part of a wider forum.

Where the poor are at home

The Pinardi chapel is an icon of Don Bosco's work. At first, it was a mere shed, unattractive, scarcely a metre and a half in height, added onto an unpretentious house.

Don Bosco had rented it for a few lire, together with the adjoining field. It would offer some shelter at least for his boys. Today, it is a chapel filled with a prayerful silence that welcomes the many eager pilgrims. Within its walls, where even the light assumes a discrete softness, love and grandeur mingle.

It suggests the Gospel paradox of weakness that testifies to divine power. A little room, too small to enclose the risen Christ to whom it is dedicated, unless you imagine the empty tomb, like a jewel case that emits a glorious light of divine mystery. It was here that Don Bosco put down his roots. His band of youngsters, driven from place to place because they were too noisy or too unruly, settled finally in its welcome

embrace. It was an unexpected godsend for the young, exhausted priest, who had wept and pleaded to heaven. This was the house of his dreams. Here God welcomed his children. To the right of the altar is a small statue of Mary, token of the tenderness that filled the Oratory.

This is the 'Pinardi House', with its own spiritual magic. It is Don Bosco's house, where the poor and the little ones are at home.

If the walls could tell tales of its beginnings, if the shadowy light could reveal all the pain of those early days, if everything could sing out in celebration, the pilgrim would hear the shouts of boys coming across the fields. Eyes would behold the loving kindness of the Father. Hands would join in prayer in thanksgiving for the stream of goodness that still flows from it.

God's place

Don Bosco's most pressing concern was the salvation of the young; and for him salvation was all-embracing: providing bread for today, a career for tomorrow, and a meaning for the whole of life. This threefold objective is reflected even in the very structure of Valdocco, his first foundation.

Nowadays a visitor to this house can pass through to the exhibition room where the various models show the different stages in the development of this primary foundation. It's striking to notice that each time the house grew in size, Don Bosco provided a larger place for prayer, so that within the same complex, and only a short distance from each other, you find the Pinardi chapel, the church of St Francis de Sales, and the basilica of Mary Help of Christians.

You might think that the reason for these successive buildings was the increasing numbers of boys arriving, but Don Bosco's real motive was to show that the place given to God should grow with the rest of the building.

Don Bosco's objective was not one of alternatives. It isn't bread or prayer, but both. It isn't to form upright citizens or good Christians, but both. It isn't to prepare for the future in this life or to prepare for eternal life, but both. Logically, then, the amount of space available in the house is divided equally among living quarters, work areas, and places to celebrate God, who gives us life and true growth.

This way of arranging things offers food for thought. In our own lives, do we give God the place which is due to him, or have we consigned him to some small corner of our life where we risk forgetting him altogether?

On the bridge

There are four of them, small and huddled together as though to shield themselves against the storm.

Four fragile witnesses of a rich and courageous story. They call them, *The Little Rooms* – small, narrow apartments that overlook the courtyard of Valdocco like a bridge above the deck of a ship. These are the captain's quarters, with their beam of light to remind any child, lost in the evening shadows of the oratory playground, that Don Bosco is watching over him. In the daytime, when the sun's light bathes the flagstones, you can see the vigorous vine, rich with grapes, climbing up the front of the building and reaching the windows behind which Don Bosco's mysterious dreams took place. In the yard below each one waits to catch his smile or a wave of his hand. In the first room you find the tiller, held by Don Alasontti, the bursar, keeping a firm hand and a steady eye on the finances. He has to navigate his way through a wretched storm of debts that threatens to submerge his little office. Don Bosco takes his soundings from Divine Providence, but with the wave of creditors crowding in, his floor-boards are wearing thin, as well as his seaman's patience! From time to time there's a swell of small donations or a surge of benefactors' generous gifts, but how do you get through this storm? The next room is where Don Bosco mapped out the route of his ambitious projects. This must be the one where he first gathered his new crew on 26 January 1854 – four trusted young men, equipped as he had dreamt, hanging on to the prophetic words of Don Bosco and ready to set sail on the seas of adventure. They named their ship '*Salesians*'.

There, too, set up prominently, like a ship's beam that the captain would never be without, is the small, cryptic inscription: *Da mihi animas, caetera tolle* (Give me souls. Nothing else matters). The two other rooms were successively Don Bosco's private apartments. He used the first one until his successor, Don Rua, finally took his place. He moved into the second one for the last two years of his life, and died there on 31 January 1888. He was on his way to an eternal rendezvous, leaving a message for his close friends on the shore: *I am leaving you here on earth, but only for a short while. Let us hope that through God's infinite goodness, we shall all meet again one day in Eternity. I shall wait for you there.*

Like a beating heart

Don't we all have 'Valdoccos' in our lives? Mere nothings that later assume great importance; small steps here and there that lead to a change of direction or a new incentive; insignificant choices made on the spur of the moment that reveal fresh light and understanding. Like this modest home, in this modest neighbourhood, that becomes the nerve-centre of a worldwide enterprise.

Yes, a true home: with a door open to welcome someone with nowhere to go; with walls to shelter and restore confidence; with a roof to protect against storm and adversity; with a table to offer a warm, welcome bowl of soup; with beds to rest in from the labours of the day; with a chapel to find prayer that brings joy to the heart and strength for the journey; with a playground to have fun with friends; with classrooms and workshops to prepare for life.

A home, like a smile you remember with warmth and joy. A home, like a shelter where you can feel at home, just when, outside, you feel a stranger. A home, like a hand extended in welcome, when you arrive worn out, then set out again stronger and braver. A home, like a landmark that provides a base and points the way ahead.

A motherhouse, like a beating heart. From this home have gone forth priests and educators to find young people for whom there has been no welcome, no joy, no education and no meaning to life. To this home come many from around the world to drink from an ever-flowing stream of love.

At the clear fountain

It has been there for a long time, surely since the beginning, guarded by its bronze lion, pouring its clear water into the stone basin. It murmurs softly, to those who are thirsty for life, that there is pure water and that it has no price. Would you know how to listen to it, you who today pass absentmindedly, without being aware? The fountain would tell you about the laughter of children who have lived here these hundred years and more, the joys but also the fears of Don Bosco, and the beginnings of Valdocco... this would take a miracle, and he believed in it. Well, yes! The fountain was there to soften the dry bread on days when there was little milk, to soothe the injuries of boys scraped at play, to quench their thirst and sometimes to wipe their eyes. Learn how to stop and moisten your own lips with its ever-fresh water.

"All you who are thirsty, come, I am the wellspring!"

Up against the wall of the Pinardi household there was a water pump, a fountain where the children came have a drink. It w a place where peop met each other an shared their little daily concerns.

Mary in our lives

You mustn't pay any attention to dreams, says John's grandmother, after listening to the nine-year-old's dream of the night before. In this dream, Mary, who appears as a shepherdess, asks him to take care of her wayward children. Just a passing dream ... yet the same episode recurs in John Bosco's life, like a short story with several twists. As the years go by, these dreams are like arranged meetings with the Lady.

On three occasions, she shows him the place where his mission will begin: an area with a bad reputation where three churches, of different sizes, will be built. Later on, she hands him a ribbon on which is written the word, *Obedience*. Faced with the problem of his priest-helpers leaving him, Mary advises him to found a congregation.

As regards the founding of the Institute of the Salesian Sisters, Mary has to insist with Don Bosco, since, whenever young women approach him about this, his answer is: I *have no time for that.*

I can't do anything for you. When the Lady repeats her request, Don Bosco finally capitulates to Mary.

Don Bosco will tell his young people all about Mary and invite them to have confidence in her, saying that Mary is not distant from them and their concerns. Rather, she is an active presence in their life, in their studies, in their recreation, in their festive celebrations, and especially when they have problems. He is at pains to explain to them that Mary is not just the person we honour in the Magnificat. She pays attention to the progress of each one, helping the *lowly*, those who are rejected, to find their rightful place. It's in this spirit that Dominic Savio and his friends form the Company of the Immaculate, a group who meet both to pray and to give practical help to any boy in the Oratory who is struggling. At the end of his life Don Bosco will say of the Lady: *She is the one who did it all.*

Mary in our lives

Throughout history Mary has been invoked as Advocate, Auxiliatrix, Help and Mediator, Help of Christians, The Immaculate …. So many titles! Yet for Mary herself only one thing filled her hopes: the coming of the Messiah, the one who would bring freedom to the people of Israel. In her own life she would always be close to her Son, first as he grew up, then in the course of his ministry. She would not always understand things, but she would carry all her experiences in her heart before God.

Our lives are marked by experiences that get the better of us – death, suffering, illness…. Often we live through them as though God were totally uninvolved. *We ask, Where is God in all that? Why believe in him if he does nothing?*

In his time Jesus faced a thousand and one situations of human suffering, but he did not eliminate them all. He walked with people, encouraged them, spent some time with them, however brief, listened to them, and sent them on their way with a new understanding of their life.

At the foot of the Cross Mary took to heart Jesus' last words to her: *Woman, this is your son*. Then his words to the disciple he loved: *This is your mother*. It was as she was living through the trauma of her son's death that he invited her to look beyond this ordeal and welcome her new mission: to be the mother of the whole human race.

Like any mother, caring for her children, Mary is our teacher. She invites us to accept the uncertainties of life, even to be thrown by them, and still to continue our earthly pilgrim way. She asks us to make good use of our gifts and to use them for the benefit of our brothers and sisters. In this way we are living proof that the Kingdom of God is here, at the heart of our lives. We must let her words to the servants at the wedding feast of Cana resonate in us: *Do whatever he tells you*. Mary followed Jesus closely to the end, and she sends us to him: he is the God who frees us from the 'every-man-for-himself' culture of today, in order to be in complete solidarity with all those around us.

He brings me children every day

Mama Margaret treads gingerly by the hearth as she tends to the cauldron sitting on the fire. The cold always bites a little more at nightfall, and she's waiting for her son who'll be home late tonight. He's in the city trying to drum up more benefactors for his work. It's January 1855. The latest building work is finished, but money is running out! A good bowl of hot soup will do him good. The old lady sits and ponders for a while. There are 88 boarders in the house now. *I've always had children*, she thinks, with a faint smile on her face. Pictures of her own sons seem to dance before her eyes, now half-closed. Is it the flames of the fire that make them glow with warm colours, or is it just a mother's love? *Anthony, Francis's son from his first marriage. I needed such a lot of patience with him. So abrasive – I could read it in his eyes – and anything I said or did rarely managed to calm him. Yet I loved him as if he were my own child.* She pokes the fire gently, though her mind is elsewhere. *He died at the Becchi six years ago. Such a sturdy man, with a wife and children, and only forty-one!*

He often came here and brought news from thereabouts. Anthony …. She gives a deep sigh and whispers a quiet prayer.
Then she remembers Joseph's laugh: *Ah, Joseph … he's a good sort! A calming influence. He takes after his father – generous, hard-working…. Then there's John. Dear John, such a mixture of bubbling energy and sensitivity. A priest-son who will never provide me with grandchildren.* Mama Margaret just laughs out loud at the thought. *After all, doesn't he bring me children every day!* She stands up and puts another log on the fire. They are poor at Valdocco, really poor. But she has no regrets. *I could have ended my days like a queen over yonder at the Becchi, surrounded by grandchildren who would have spoiled me. But I chose to be with John. Quite ironical, really: I was the one who asked him to leave home when he was twelve; then one day he came to take me by the hand and bring me here! Dear John… Mary, protect him! He's so fragile.* Fatigue gradually takes over. An hour or two later, John returns to find her fast asleep by the fireside.

Singing and laughing, running and praying ...

In September 1845 the eight-year-old Michael Rua meets Don Bosco for the first time. He still hasn't got over his father's death, and since then his mother allows him to go to the Oratory from time to time, as long as he's careful to avoid bad companions!

- *Mum, they're going to Superga today.*
- *You'll enjoy that. It's a wonderful place.*
Here, take a packed lunch, and be careful.

Like a shot, he's on his way. Fortunately, they live quite near to the Filippi field. In no time at all he's there with his friends, and judging by the noise there's a big crowd this Sunday. He scarcely has time to say 'Hello' to the young clerics and join a group playing quoits before a roll on a big drum and a trumpet blast call them together. They take up the stilts, the bowls, etc., and Don Bosco tells them it's time to set off. He gives just one piece of advice: be calm and orderly going through the city streets, so as to give a good impression to everyone.

At the foot of the hill leading to the basilica, a fine young horse is waiting. Don Bosco mounts it, and tells them the latest news. Don Borel, the chaplain, prepared the horse. He's waiting for them up there. *If you're too tired to make it, put your hand up!* In reply the boys clap, shout and sing their heads off! Some take the horse by its ears, some by its nose or its tail, and generally give horse and rider a rough ride! What a cacophony, as the drum beats

out a marching rhythm, trumpet and guitar provide the 'music', only to be drowned out by the raucous voices, laughing, joking and shouting, before they finally arrive, drenched in perspiration. They come together in the courtyard of the basilica, where they get their breath back and Don Bosco tells them the history of this wonderful sanctuary, which also houses an Academy. Soon the president arrives on the scene and invites them all to a picnic! The afternoon is free for games or a tour of the sanctuary. As usual on a Sunday, fashionable society people begin to arrive, and towards four o'clock Don Bosco gives a short sermon in the basilica, followed by a popular hymn.

Afterwards, the boys run to the balustrades and release balloons that float down towards the city, everyone giving a running commentary on his own balloon. Then it's thanks to all concerned, and the walk back down to Turin, again with songs, laughter and running helter-skelter. Occasionally, too, there are prayers. Once in the city they begin gradually to leave the main party and make their way home, and seven or eight of the bigger, stronger boys carry the games equipment. What a great outing it has been! Michael Rua is one of the last to leave Don Bosco – maybe next year he'll be able to give a hand! Much later, after the death of Don Bosco, Michael Rua will take his place as head of the Salesian Society.

When the well runs dry

The world has gone mad. The pace is too fast. To find your place in life, it's a rat race: you win or you lose. Everyone's in a hurry, and there's no time to think or dream. The world has turned grey. The sky is far away, beyond a wall of concrete.

Sometimes we feel a yearning to escape and find something different. We'd like to drop our baggage of problems, just leave them there and go away. We want to shake off this sensation that we are overwhelmed and helpless; this feeling that there's no point any more in what we do from day to day. The well has run dry.

To lose the taste for water that should be a spring of life is worse than being parched with thirst. It's then that we have to find another well to drink from. That well can be for us a significant place, a pleasant activity, a time of prayer and meditation, an unexpected change that makes us refocus on what is essential. When we find that our heart and mind are no longer in what we are doing, we need to rediscover our personal wholeness.

Don Bosco's autumn walks put oxygen into the lungs of the Oratory boys – got them away, gave them a change of scene that sent them home with a new zest for life. For us it can be a short retreat, an unexpected treat, some time off with friends. Like holiday-makers coming home with a healthy tan, we can find that it's our inner person that has got colour back: in our faith, our love, our hope, our life.

Canon Joseph Cottolengo *(1786 - 1842)*

It was February 1842, and as in every other year, Don Joseph Cafasso would be sure to send some of his young priest students from the Ecclesiastical College, the 'Convitto'. Canon Cottolengo depended greatly on this providential help for the sick – people in wretched conditions who came to him for care and comfort. Among them were those abandoned in the street, epileptics, deaf-mutes, and people with severe physical or mental handicaps. An immense number needing protection and treatment! The Canon had launched this heroic work fifteen years earlier, and was now at the point of exhaustion. Was it an act of folly, or some over-reaching ambition of his? He had gone ahead depending totally and solely on Divine Providence. The Ministry of Finance and even King Charles Albert himself had had a close look at his work – men of influence, concern and perception, who wanted to ensure that it would go on. But this man of God from Chieri was one of those prophetic figures who follow the gospel precept of love to the letter and will have it no other way. One September day in 1827 he had witnessed the death of a young French woman, Jeanne-Marie Gonnet, who was travelling with her husband and three young children. She had been refused admission by all the hospitals in Turin - arcane administration, the poverty of the family, and so many futile arguments when she was at death's door! His mind was made up: *I was sick and you visited me. I was a stranger and you welcomed me,* says the Gospel. It was time to transform good will into action! With gifts and loans he was able to open a small hospital in the city centre and later moved to a site near the main market and close to the Marchioness Barolo's establishment. When the priests from the College came, Joseph Cottolengo gave them a warm welcome. Seeing Don Bosco among them, he said: *You have a good head. Come and help at the Little House. You won't be short of work.*

The Consolata

Where does this rare fragrance of grace and love come from? It pervades the city, blending the bitterness of daily suffering with the sweetness of divine mercy. Just follow that little lady, shuffling along, or this modest gentleman with his steady pace, or that little family locked in grief – all of them drawn by a common faith towards the sanctuary of the Consolata. It appears that long ago, in the fourth century, the Virgin Mary planted a rose in the city to ease the sufferings of her children. Since then, the greatest architects, sculptors and painters, Guarini, Juvarra, Crosato, Alberoni, Ceppi and many others have been approached over the centuries, as skilled gardeners to beautify the building and give it its final structure. Today, its side chapels are like so many cells of a choice honeycomb that everyone comes to at least once in a lifetime. Every day, from early morning, they come from the city and the surrounding countryside like so many worker bees and quietly enter the church. There they lay down the pollen of their burdens, whether it be from long night hours with a sick child, from bitter exchanges that are tearing a couple apart, or from oppressive debts that threaten a family's future. So many raw wounds, though often hidden from view, and all are laid at the feet of their consoling Queen. A painful task, but devoutly done, trusting in the perpetual miracle of love that will transform this pulp of bitter pain into sweet, copious honey that will strengthen the human heart. Don Bosco would come here often, full of confidence: the young student in Chieri, his heart bursting with joy; the new priest, with a grateful heart, the day after his ordination; the sorrowing son, bathed in tears in the small hours of 25 November 1856, grieving for Mama Margaret, the mother he had just lost. The garden of this city holds a secret flower, whose fragrance refreshes the human spirit and restores its warmth and colour. Everyone knows its name: the 'Consolata'.

Epilogue

90

A contagious hope

The noise level in the city has risen. No longer do the sounds of carriage wheels or the cries of the market stallholders fill the air. Today there's dense traffic. The city is larger and its population more numerous. But sadly, the poor are still there. Industrial progress has its casualties, even if the resulting poverty is at a personal rather than a material level, and often less visible.

If you pass through the Valdocco sector today, you find that it is no longer the suburb of the past. It is now an integral part of the city, which has sprawled even farther still. Moreover, it is popular and cosmopolitan, even if it has refused the face-lifts urged by the city authorities. Its faded facades and uneven pavements are still there. You almost expect to meet a cassocked priest making his rounds, looking for titbits of news, asking for alms, patting children on the head, or even doing some sleight-of-hand for a group of teenagers. You can almost hear them laughing.

Yes, you find yourself thinking of Don Bosco and what has become of his dream at the age of nine. He saw the Valdocco house grow to welcome more and more children. He founded two religious congregations and mobilised many people to carry on his expanding work.

His dream took him beyond frontiers for yet further development. The men and women who have thrown in their lot with him are many thousands, and they are at the service of young people across the world. Inevitably, as the field of labour extends, the needs become greater. Though there are many hands to the task, more are needed.

We have been to the very roots of a dream and now we are witnessing its outspread branches. As we went through the various stages of Don Bosco's life, it made us reflect on our own. We can be sure of this : God has a dream for each one of us. He calls us to take a road where we shall find happiness. We fulfil this dream through a series of small choices. As we learn from Don Bosco, once we set our sights on it, we don't let obstacles and difficulties loom large. The important thing is to make a start and then keep going. He said of himself that he went ahead to the point of foolishness.

Don Bosco is a saint, not because of the challenges he faced and overcame, nor because of the miracles he worked. His sanctity consists in being faithful, come what may, to the God-given mission he undertook. Faith was his strength, love was his gift, and his hope is his inspiration to others. Like him, may we always believe, love and hope!

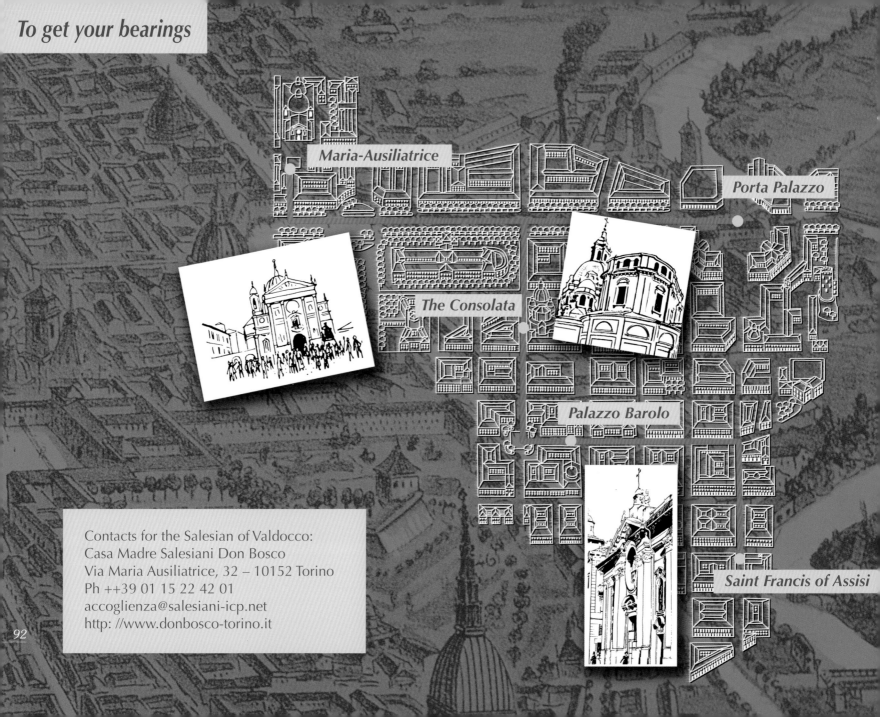

Maria-Ausiliatrice

Porta Palazzo

The Consolata

Palazzo Barolo

Saint Francis of Assisi

Contacts for the Salesian of Valdocco:
Casa Madre Salesiani Don Bosco
Via Maria Ausiliatrice, 32 – 10152 Torino
Ph ++39 01 15 22 42 01
accoglienza@salesiani-icp.net
http://www.donbosco-torino.it

Turin

Castelnuovo

Chieri

Mondonio

The Becchi
Colle Don Bosco

Morialdo

Capriglio

Contacts for the Salesian of Becchi:
Colle Don Bosco
Ph ++39 01 19 92 71 58
info@colledonbosco.it
http: //www.colledonbosco.it

93

Bibliography

Books

Don Bosco
Teresio Bosco
Éditions Don Bosco
Biography in two versions (long and short)

Don Bosco, l'aventure d'une vie
L'Atelier Multimédia
Beautiful album, richly illustrated
Out of print: Contact Maisons Don Bosco

La vie de Don Bosco
Francis Desramaut
Éditions Don Bosco
A well-documented, historical approach

Petite vie de Don Bosco
Robert Schiélé
Desclée de Brouwer
Story (137 pages)

Don Bosco et la Famille Salésienne
Morand Wirth
Éditions Don Bosco
Historical and spiritual study of the development of the Salesian Family from 1815 to our own time (620 pages)

Prier avec Don Bosco
Daniel Federspiel
Éditions du Signe
Booklet of prayers united with Don Bosco (45 pages)

Comic book

La vie prodigieuse et héroïque de Don Bosco
Jigé
Éditions Don Bosco
The famous comic book

Videos

Saint Jean Bosco, une pédagogie pour le XXIᵉ siècle
Jour du Seigneur - Laurence Chartier
CFRT – France2, Coll. Voir & Dire
Commentary presenting Don Bosco and his world, with the testimonies of Jean-Marie Petitclerc, of young educators at Valdocco and of Salesian Cooperators (30')

Don Bosco, l'ami de la jeunesse
CAT Productions (available at La Procure)
Commentary on the life and world of Don Bosco (52')

Don Bosco
Film by Leandro Castellani
Éditions Don Bosco (DVD)
The film which appeared in Italian movie theaters in 1988

À l'école de Don Bosco
L'Atelier Multimédia
Éditions Don Bosco (DVD)
Video with a pedagogical theme for teams of educators

CD-Rom (Mac-PC)

Don Bosco, l'ami des jeunes
L'Atelier Multimédia
Éditions Don Bosco
Biographical view, with a «History Journal» to situate events in their context, and with accounts of the present situation of the Salesian mission.

La pédagogie salésienne de A à Z
Atelier Multimédia
Éditions Don Bosco
Organized by key words, content enriched by short interviews. Texts with printable reference. Out of stock but will be reprinted to meet demand.

These places speak to us

Credits

Concept and production: L'Atelier Multimédia (www.donboscomedia.com)
(Jean-Noël Charmoille, Daniel Federspiel, Vincent Grodziski, Bernard Hubler, Jacques Rey)

Graphic design and layout: Jacques Rey

Texts:
Daniel Federspiel pp. 10-18-20-24-26-28-34-37-40-42-44-46-48-50-52-54-60-61-62-64-66-67-74-76-78-84-86-88-89
Jean-Noël Charmoille pp. 6-25-27-29-30-41-43-47-49-51-53-68-69-73-77-79-87-91
Bernard Hubler pp. 5-8-12-15-17-38-57-70-72 — Jacques Rey pp. 6-14-19-21-32-58
Vincent Grodziski pp. 65-71-82-83 — Jean-François Meurs p. 11 — Annie Garcin p. 80 — Théo Mertens p. 22

Drawings:
Jacques Rey pp. 24-27-43-70-72-76-88-89 — Nino Musio p. 5 — Sr. Ludgera, Monastery of Reute (Tapestry) p. 80 — Batick, Monastery of Sainte Lioba pp. 6-19 — Leopoldo Espáriz p. 37 — Bas relief in bronze by Consuelo Mels Colloredo p. 61 and back cover — Archives of the city of Turin pp. 82-92 — Domingo Bladé p. 90 — Sculptures by Professor Giovanni Dragoni pp. 32-33.

Photo Credits:
Jacques Rey pp. 1-2-4-7-8-9-11-13-19-21-22-23-24 (top of the page)-29-31 (top of the page)-32 (bottom of the page)-33 (background)-34-36-37-40-41-45-46-47-48-49-52-56-57-58-62-64-65-67-70-71-74-75-78-79-80-81-83-85-87-90-93-95 — LDC-Guerrino Pera pp. 14-15-24-25-26-27 (bottom of the page)-32-33-38-39-42-43-54-55-59 (top of the page)-65-76-77 — Colle Don Bosco pp. 13 (full page)-30-31(bottom of the page) — Salesian Archives pp. 16-17-35 (black and white photos by De Agonstini)-47 (photo sepia) - Anton Birklbauer p. 61 and back cover - RMN. Hervé Lewandowski, Musée du Louvre, Paris p. 68 — Hulton Picture Library p. 69 — Photodisc p. 50 — Group of religious philately p. 88 — *Front cover:* Jacques Rey, LDC, Colle Don Bosco.

Thanks:
To the Elledici, to the Community of the Colle Don Bosco and to the Don Bosco Missions of Turin for their valuable assistance.

For more information about Don Bosco and the Salesians, you can contact:

Œuvres et Missions de Don Bosco
393, bis rue des Pyrénées
75020 Paris
Tel 01 47 97 51 21
Email: province@donboscofrance.com
Web site: www.salesien.com

Éditions du Signe
1, rue Alfred Kastler
B.P. 94 – ECKBOLSHEIM
67038 STRASBOURG Cedex 2
France
Tel. ++ 33 (0)3 88 78 91 91 – Fax ++ 33 (0)3 88 78 91 99
© Éditions du Signe 2008
ISBN: 978-2-7468-2216-0